# perfect
# rice & risotto

This is a Parragon Publishing book
First published in 2006

Parragon Publishing
Queen Street House
4 Queen Street
Bath BA1 1HE, UK

Copyright © Parragon Books Ltd 2006
Designed by Terry Jeavons & Company

ISBN 1-40547-403-3

Printed in China

This book uses imperial, metric, and US cup measurements. Follow the same units of measurement throughout; do not mix imperial and metric. All spoon measurements are level, unless otherwise stated: teaspoons are assumed to be 5ml, and tablespoons are assumed to be 15ml. Unless otherwise stated, milk is assumed to be whole, eggs and individual fruits such as bananas are medium, and pepper is freshly ground black pepper.

Recipes using raw or very lightly cooked eggs should be avoided by infants, the elderly, pregnant women, convalescents, and anyone suffering from an illness. Pregnant and breast-feeding women are advised to avoid eating peanuts and peanut products.

# perfect
# rice &
# risotto

# introduction

Rice is one of those "staple" foods that really earns the description. It's a very healthy, lowfat, nutritious grain that takes only minutes to cook and lends itself to endless treatments. It is used all over the world, so there is an incredible diversity of recipes to choose from, giving such different results that you will probably forget they are all based on rice!

Another major point to commend rice as part of your diet is the fact that it comes neatly packaged, fits conveniently into your store cupboard, and can remain there for around a year without any loss of quality. This means that you can always have something on hand

to serve as a simple side dish, with a touch of butter or olive oil added and perhaps a little flavoring such as lime zest, chopped herbs, or spices, or to use as the base for your main dish, in whatever cultural style you fancy!

Rice comes in many varieties, and it is important to use the correct type for the recipe you are making. East Asian recipes use long-grain rice, which is often fragranced with jasmine in Thailand, and a glutinous variety which is excellent for desserts. Indian Basmati rice has a distinctive aroma and is sold in brown (unpolished) and white (polished) forms. Rice grown in the United States is long-grain and has many uses. In Italy, where risotto is a favorite dish, and Spain, where rice is the base for paella, the rice is plump—when making either of these dishes, it is essential to use the authentic rice.

For maximum nutritional value, choose unpolished brown rice, which is often favored by vegetarians for its high vitamin B content.

Other types to try are wild rice, a black long-grain rice with a gorgeously chewy texture that works wonderfully with white rice in salads, and the nutty-flavored red rice grown in the Camargue in France.

Whatever cuisine you choose, you will be bound to enjoy it!

# soups &
# light meals

Rice is the perfect starting point for a light meal. It is very quick to cook, so if you are rushing around at the weekend or exhausted after a day at work you can still have a satisfying, nourishing meal without devoting too much time and energy to its preparation. And it's very easy to digest, so it's excellent for lunch or a late supper because it doesn't leave you with a heavy, bloated feeling in the middle of the day or just before bedtime. If you have a gluten intolerance, rice is an excellent alternative to pasta for a speedy meal.

Soups made with a little rice added are an excellent start—the rice provides a little bit of "bite" so that you feel satisfied. A simple risotto takes less than half an hour to make but looks and tastes very impressive, so if you are having friends round, give them a fresh-tasting Lemon and Rosemary Risotto, or a Sunshine Risotto—on a cold day, this will really remind you of better weather to come, as will a Cashew Nut Paella.

Stir-frying, the method of cooking favored in East and Southeast Asia, has come to be recognized as an exceptionally healthy way to produce a meal, as the ingredients are cooked so quickly as to preserve all their nutritional value. Try Chicken Fried Rice when you need a boost—there's plenty of goodness there!

# lamb & rice soup

## ingredients

**SERVES 4**

5$^1$/$_2$ oz/150 g lean lamb

salt

1$^1$/$_4$ oz/50 g/scant $^1$/$_4$ cup rice

1$^1$/$_2$ pints/850 ml/3$^1$/$_2$ cups
    lamb stock

1 leek, sliced

1 garlic clove, thinly sliced

2 tsp light soy sauce

1 tsp rice wine vinegar

1 medium open-cap
    mushroom, thinly sliced

## method

**1** Using a sharp knife, trim any visible fat from the lamb and cut the meat into thin strips. Set aside until required.

**2** Bring a large pan of lightly salted water to a boil and add the rice. Return to a boil, stir once, reduce the heat, and cook for 10–15 minutes, or until tender. Drain the cooked rice, rinse under cold running water, drain again, and set aside.

**3** Place the lamb stock in a large pan and bring to a boil. Add the lamb strips, leek, garlic, soy sauce, and rice wine vinegar, reduce the heat, cover, and let simmer for 10 minutes, or until the lamb is tender and cooked through.

**4** Add the mushroom slices and cooked rice to the pan and cook for an additional 2–3 minutes, or until the mushrooms are completely cooked through. Ladle the soup into 4 warmed bowls and serve immediately.

# pork with rice & egg soup

## ingredients

**SERVES 4**

12 oz pork loin, skin on

2 tsp chili paste

3 oz/85 g/scant $^1/_2$ cup
   jasmine rice

$1^1/_2$ pints/850 ml/$3^1/_2$ cups
   chicken stock

1 tbsp Thai red curry paste

1 tsp shrimp paste

2 lemongrass stalks, snapped
   in half

2-inch piece fresh gingerroot,
   sliced thinly

2 eggs

4 scallions, chopped

2 fresh red chiles, sliced

4 sprigs of fresh Thai basil

## method

**1** Cut the skin away from the meat and peel back. Spread with chili paste, then fold the skin back over the meat. Place in a roasting pan and roast in a preheated oven, 400°F/200°C, for 40–45 minutes, until crisp and browned. Slice the meat thickly and then cut into thin strips. Chop the crackling. Set aside.

**2** Meanwhile, rinse the rice in cold water several times until the water remains clear. Drain well.

**3** Pour the stock into a pan, add the curry paste, shrimp paste, lemongrass, and gingerroot, and bring to a boil. Add the rice and bring back to a boil. Reduce the heat and let simmer for 10–12 minutes.

**4** Break the eggs into the soup and, once they start to set, break the yolks and stir through the rice. Let simmer for an additional 3–4 minutes, until the rice is cooked. Stir in the scallions and chiles. Ladle into warmed bowls and serve topped with the hot sliced pork and pieces of crackling. Garnish with the basil sprigs.

# tomato, rice & tarragon soup

## ingredients

**SERVES 4**

2 tbsp olive oil

2 garlic cloves, chopped

2 red onions, chopped

1 red bell pepper, seeded and
   chopped

8 tomatoes, skinned, seeded
   and chopped

$1^3/_4$ pints/1 liter/4 cups
   vegetable stock

1 celery stalk, trimmed
   and sliced

6 oz/175 g/generous
   $^3/_4$ cup brown rice

1 tbsp chopped fresh tarragon

salt and pepper

$3^1/_2$ fl oz/100 ml/scant $^1/_2$ cup
   heavy cream

sprigs of fresh tarragon,
   to garnish

fresh crusty bread, to serve

## method

**1** Heat the oil in a large pan. Add the garlic and onions and cook over medium heat, stirring, for 3 minutes, until slightly softened. Add the bell pepper and the tomatoes and cook for another 2 minutes, stirring. Stir in the stock, then add the celery, rice, and tarragon. Season with salt and pepper. Bring to a boil, then lower the heat and simmer for 30 minutes. Remove from the heat and let cool for 10 minutes.

**2** Transfer half of the soup into a food processor and blend until smooth. Return to the pan with the rest of the soup and cook for 5 minutes. Stir in the cream and cook for another 5 minutes. Remove from the heat and ladle into serving bowls. Garnish with sprigs of fresh tarragon and serve with fresh crusty bread.

# chinese fried rice

## ingredients

**SERVES 4**

1¹/4 pints/700 ml/
   3 cups water

¹/2 tsp salt

10¹/2 oz/300 g/1¹/2 cups
   long-grain rice

2 eggs

salt and pepper

4 tsp cold water

3 tbsp sunflower oil

4 scallions, sliced diagonally

1 red, green, or yellow bell
   pepper, cored, seeded,
   and thinly sliced

3–4 lean bacon slices, rinded
   and cut into strips

7 oz/200 g/1¹/3 cups fresh
   bean sprouts

4¹/2 oz/125g/1¹/8 cups frozen
   peas, thawed

2 tbsp soy sauce (optional)

## method

**1** Pour the water into the wok with the salt and bring to a boil. Rinse the rice in a strainer under cold running water until the water runs clear, drain thoroughly, and add to the boiling water. Stir well, then cover the wok tightly with the lid, and let simmer gently for 12–13 minutes. (Do not remove the lid during cooking or the steam will escape and the rice will not be cooked.)

**2** Remove the lid, give the rice a good stir, and spread out on a large plate or baking sheet to cool and dry.

**3** Meanwhile, beat each egg separately with salt and pepper and 2 teaspoons of cold water. Heat 1 tablespoon of oil in a preheated wok, pour in the first egg, swirl it around, and let cook undisturbed until set. Transfer to a cutting board and cook the second egg. Cut the omelets into thin slices.

**4** Add the remaining oil to the wok and when really hot stir-fry the scallions and bell pepper for 1–2 minutes. Add the bacon and continue to stir-fry for an additional 2 minutes. Add the bean sprouts and peas and toss together thoroughly. Stir in the soy sauce, if using.

**5** Add the rice and salt and pepper to taste and stir-fry for 1 minute, then add the strips of omelet and continue to stir-fry for 2 minutes, or until the rice is piping hot. Serve immediately.

# italian rice & peas

## ingredients

SERVES 4

1³/₄ pints/1 liter/4 cups
    chicken or vegetable stock
3 oz/85 g butter
3 shallots, chopped finely
4 oz/115 g pancetta or
    rindless lean bacon, diced
10 oz/280 g/scant 1¹/₄ cups
    Arborio rice
5 fl oz/150 ml/²/₃ cup
    dry white wine
8 oz/225 g/1¹/₂ cups peas,
    thawed if frozen
salt and pepper
Parmesan cheese shavings,
    to garnish

## method

**1** Pour the stock into a large pan and bring to a boil. Reduce the heat and let simmer gently.

**2** Melt 2 oz/55 g of the butter in another large, heavy-bottom pan. Add the shallots and pancetta or bacon and cook over low heat, stirring occasionally, for 5 minutes, until the shallots are softened. Add the rice and cook, stirring constantly, for 2–3 minutes, until all the grains are thoroughly coated and glistening.

**3** Pour in the wine and cook, stirring constantly, until it has almost completely evaporated. Add a ladleful of hot stock and cook, stirring constantly, until all the stock has been absorbed. Continue cooking and adding the stock, a ladleful at a time, for about 10 minutes.

**4** Add the peas, then continue adding the stock, a ladleful at a time, for an additional 10 minutes, or until the rice is tender and the liquid has been absorbed.

**5** Stir in the remaining butter and season to taste with salt and pepper. Transfer the risotto to a warmed serving dish, garnish with Parmesan shavings, and serve immediately.

# shredded spinach & ham risotto

## ingredients

### SERVES 4

1³/4 pints/1 liter/4 cups
   simmering chicken stock
   (see method)
8 oz/225 g/5 cups fresh
   young spinach leaves
4 oz/115 g cooked ham
1 tbsp olive oil
3 tbsp butter
1 small onion,
   finely chopped
10 oz/280 g/1¹/2 cups
   Arborio rice
5 fl oz/150 ml/²/3 cup
   dry white wine
2 fl oz/150 ml/¹/4 cup
   light cream
3 oz/85 g/³/4 cup freshly grated
   Parmesan or
   Grana Padano cheese
salt and pepper

## method

**1** Bring the stock to a boil in a pan, then reduce the heat and keep simmering gently over low heat while you are cooking the risotto.

**2** Wash the spinach well and slice into thin shreds. Cut the ham into thin strips.

**3** Heat the oil with 2 tablespoons of the butter in a deep pan over medium heat until the butter has melted. Add the onion and cook, stirring occasionally, for 5 minutes, or until soft and starting to turn golden. Do not brown. Reduce the heat, add the rice, and mix to coat in oil and butter. Cook, stirring constantly, for 2–3 minutes, or until the grains are translucent. Add the wine and cook, stirring constantly, for 1 minute until reduced.

**4** Gradually add the hot stock, a ladleful at a time. Stir constantly and add more liquid as the rice absorbs each addition. Increase the heat to medium so that the liquid bubbles. Cook for 20 minutes, or until all the liquid is absorbed and the rice is creamy. Add the spinach and ham with the last ladleful of stock.

**5** Remove the risotto from the heat and add the remaining butter and the cream. Mix well, then stir in the Parmesan until it melts. Season to taste and serve at once.

# rice with chorizo & shrimp

## ingredients

**SERVES 4**

2 tbsp olive oil

1 large onion, chopped

1 red bell pepper, cored,
    seeded, and chopped

1 green bell pepper, cored,
    seeded, and chopped

2 large garlic cloves, crushed

1 large tomato, chopped

7 oz/200 g/scant 1 cup
    easy-cook Spanish rice

salt and pepper

7 oz chorizo sausage, cut into
    $1^1/_4$-in. slices,
    casings removed

16fl oz/450 ml/2 cups
    vegetable, fish, or
    chicken stock

1 lb/450 g large uncooked
    shrimp, shelled and
    deveined

2 tbsp finely chopped fresh
    parsley, to garnish

## method

**1** Heat the oil in a large, lidded skillet over medium–high heat. Add the onion and bell peppers and cook for 2 minutes. Add the garlic and continue cooking, stirring occasionally, for 3 minutes, or until the onion and bell peppers are soft, but not brown.

**2** Add the tomato, rice, and salt and pepper to taste and continue cooking for 2 minutes.

**3** Stir in the chorizo, then the stock and bring to a boil. Reduce the heat to low, cover, and let simmer for 15 minutes until the rice is tender, but still moist.

**4** Stir in the shrimp, cover, and cook for about 5 minutes until they turn pink and the liquid has been absorbed: if the rice remains too moist, let simmer for an additional 2 minutes, uncovered. Taste and adjust the seasoning if necessary. Sprinkle with parsley and serve.

# chicken fried rice

## ingredients

**SERVES 4**

$1/2$ tbsp sesame oil

6 shallots, peeled and cut
  into fourths

1 lb/450 g cooked, cubed
  chicken meat

3 tbsp soy sauce

2 carrots, diced

1 celery stalk, diced

1 yellow bell pepper, diced

6 oz/175 g/$1^{1}/2$ cups fresh
  peas

$3^{1}/2$ oz/100 g canned corn

$9^{1}/2$ oz/275 g/$3^{2}/3$ cups
  cooked long-grain rice

2 large eggs, scrambled

## method

**1** Heat the oil in a large skillet over a medium heat. Add the shallots and cook until soft, then add the chicken and 2 tablespoons of the soy sauce and stir-fry for 5–6 minutes.

**2** Stir in the carrots, celery, yellow bell pepper, peas, and corn and stir-fry for another 5 minutes. Add the rice and stir thoroughly.

**3** Finally, stir in the scrambled eggs and the remaining tablespoon of soy sauce. Serve immediately.

# fish brunch

## ingredients

**SERVES 4–6**

3¹/₂ oz/100 g/¹/₂ cup
   brown rice
a few saffron threads
10¹/₂ oz/300 g undyed
   smoked haddock fillets
1 bay leaf
1 large onion
5 fl oz/150 ml/²/₃ cup milk
4 oz/115 g green beans,
   chopped
2 tbsp olive oil
1–2 garlic cloves, crushed
5 fl oz/150 ml/²/₃ cup
   fish stock
4 oz/115 g/scant ³/₄ cup corn
   kernels, thawed if frozen
2 tomatoes, chopped
8 oz/225 g raw jumbo shrimp,
   shelled
salt and pepper
1 tbsp chopped fresh cilantro

## method

**1** Cook the rice in a pan of lightly salted boiling water with the saffron for 25 minutes, or until tender. Drain and set aside.

**2** Meanwhile, rinse the haddock and put into a skillet with the bay leaf. Cut a few slices off the onion and add to the skillet. Pour over the milk and bring to a boil, then reduce the heat and let simmer for 10 minutes, or until the fish is cooked. Drain and let cool slightly. When cool enough to handle, remove and discard the skin and any remaining bones and flake the flesh into small pieces.

**3** Cook the beans in a pan of lightly salted boiling water for 5 minutes, drain, then plunge into cold water. Drain again and set aside.

**4** Finely chop the remaining onion. Heat the oil in a large skillet over medium heat, add the onion and garlic, and cook for 5 minutes, stirring frequently. Add the cooked rice, stock, haddock, beans, corn, tomatoes, and jumbo shrimp. Cook, stirring occasionally, for 10 minutes, or until the shrimp are cooked and have turned pink. Add salt and pepper to taste, stir in the cilantro, and serve.

# radicchio risotto

## ingredients

**SERVES 6–8**

1 large head of radicchio,
    outer damaged leaves
    removed
2 tbsp corn or other
    vegetable oil
2 tbsp butter
4 oz/115 g pancetta
    or thick-cut smoked
    bacon, diced
1 large onion, finely chopped
1 garlic clove, finely chopped
14 oz/400 g/scant 2 cups
    Arborio rice
$2^{3}/_{4}$ pints/1.5 liters/scant
    $6^{1}/_{2}$ cups simmering
    chicken or vegetable stock
    (see page 18)
2 fl oz/50 ml/$^{1}/_{4}$ cup
    heavy cream
2 oz/55 g/$^{1}/_{2}$ cup freshly
    grated Parmesan cheese
3–4 tbsp chopped fresh
    flat-leaf parsley
salt and pepper

## method

**1** Cut the radicchio head in half lengthwise and remove the triangular core. Place the halves cut-side down and shred finely. Set aside.

**2** Heat the oil and butter in a large, heavy-bottom pan over medium heat. Add the pancetta and cook, stirring occasionally, for 3–4 minutes until it starts to color. Add the onion and garlic and cook for 1 minute.

**3** Reduce the heat, add the rice, and mix to coat in oil and butter. Cook, stirring constantly, for 2–3 minutes or until the grains are translucent. Add the radicchio and cook, stirring for 1 minute until it just starts to wilt.

**4** Gradually add the hot stock, a ladleful at a time. Stir constantly and add more liquid as the rice absorbs each addition. Increase the heat to medium so that the liquid bubbles. Cook for 20 minutes, or until all the liquid is absorbed and the rice is creamy.

**5** Stir in the cream, Parmesan, and parsley and season to taste with salt and pepper. Remove the pan from the heat and spoon the risotto onto warmed plates. Serve at once.

# tuna rice

## ingredients

**SERVES 4**

3 tbsp peanut or corn oil

4 scallions, chopped

2 garlic cloves, finely chopped

7 oz/200 g canned tuna in oil,
    drained and flaked

6 oz/175 g frozen or canned
    corn kernels and bell
    peppers

1 lb 10 oz/750 g/$3^1/_2$ cups
    cold boiled rice

2 tbsp Thai fish sauce

1 tbsp light soy sauce

salt and pepper

2 tbsp chopped fresh cilantro,
    to garnish

## method

**1** Heat the peanut oil in a preheated wok or large, heavy-bottomed skillet. Add the scallions and stir-fry for 2 minutes, then add the garlic and stir-fry for an additional 1 minute.

**2** Add the tuna and the corn and bell peppers, and stir-fry for 2 minutes.

**3** Add the rice, fish sauce, and soy sauce and stir-fry for 2 minutes. Season to taste with salt and pepper and serve immediately, garnished with chopped cilantro.

# crab fried rice

## ingredients

SERVES 4

$5^1/2$ o/150 g/$^3/_4$ cup
    long-grain rice

salt

2 tbsp groundnut oil

125 g/$4^1/2$ oz canned white
    crab meat, drained

1 leek, sliced

150 g/$5^1/2$ oz bean sprouts

2 eggs, beaten

1 tbsp light soy sauce

2 tsp lime juice

1 tsp sesame oil

sliced lime, to garnish

## method

**1** Cook the rice in a pan of lightly salted boiling water for 15 minutes. Drain, rinse under cold running water, and drain again.

**2** Heat the oil in a preheated wok or large, heavy-bottom skillet until it is really hot. Add the crab meat, leek, and bean sprouts to the wok or skillet and stir-fry for 2–3 minutes. Remove the mixture with a slotted spoon and set aside.

**3** Add the eggs to the wok and cook, stirring occasionally, for 2–3 minutes, until they begin to set. Stir the rice and crab meat mixture into the eggs in the wok.

**4** Add the soy sauce and lime juice to the mixture in the wok. Cook for 1 minute, stirring to combine. Sprinkle with the sesame oil and toss lightly to mix. Garnish with sliced lime and serve.

# shrimp & rice salad

## ingredients

**SERVES 4**

6 oz/175 g/generous $^3/_4$ cup
   mixed long-grain
   and wild rice
12 oz/350 g cooked shelled
   shrimp
1 mango, peeled, pitted,
   and diced
4 scallions, sliced
1 oz/25 g/$^1/_4$ cup slivered
   almonds
1 tbsp finely chopped
   fresh mint
salt and pepper

## dressing

1 tbsp extra-virgin olive oil
2 tsp lime juice
1 garlic clove, crushed
1 tsp honey
salt and pepper

## method

**1** Bring a large pan of lightly salted water to a boil. Add the rice, return to a boil, and cook for 35 minutes, or until tender. Drain, then transfer to a large bowl and stir in the shrimp.

**2** To make the dressing, combine the olive oil, lime juice, garlic, and honey in a large pitcher, season to taste with salt and pepper, and whisk until well blended. Pour the dressing over the rice and shrimp mixture and let cool.

**3** Add the mango, scallions, almonds, and mint to the salad and season to taste with pepper. Stir thoroughly, transfer to a large serving dish, and serve.

# shrimp with coconut rice

## ingredients

**SERVES 4**

4 oz/115 g/1 cup dried
   Chinese mushrooms
2 tbsp vegetable or
   peanut oil
6 scallions, chopped
2 oz/55 g/scant $1/2$ cup dry
   unsweetened coconut
1 fresh green chile, seeded
   and chopped
8 oz/225 g/generous 1 cup
   jasmine rice
5 fl oz/150 ml/$2/3$ cup
   fish stock
14 fl oz/400 ml/$1^3/4$ cups
   coconut milk
12 oz/350 g cooked shelled
   shrimp
6 sprigs fresh Thai basil

## method

**1** Place the mushrooms in a small bowl, cover with hot water, and set aside to soak for 30 minutes. Drain, then cut off and discard the stalks and slice the caps.

**2** Heat 1 tablespoon of the oil in a wok and stir-fry the scallions, coconut, and chile for 2–3 minutes, until lightly browned. Add the mushrooms and stir-fry for 3–4 minutes.

**3** Add the rice and stir-fry for 2–3 minutes, then add the stock and bring to a boil. Reduce the heat and add the coconut milk. Let simmer for 10–15 minutes, until the rice is tender. Stir in the shrimp and basil, heat through, and serve.

# shrimp pilaf

## ingredients

**SERVES 4**

3 tbsp olive oil

1 onion, chopped finely

1 red bell pepper, cored,
   seeded and sliced thinly

1 garlic clove, crushed

8 oz/225 g/1$\frac{1}{3}$ cups long-
   grain white rice

1$\frac{1}{4}$ pints/700 ml/3 cups
   fish, chicken,
   or vegetable stock

1 bay leaf

salt and pepper

14 oz/400 g shelled cooked
   shrimp, thawed and
   drained if frozen

whole cooked shrimp, lemon
   wedges, and black Greek
   olives, to garnish

### to serve

grated kefalotiri or pecorino
   cheese

cubes of authentic Greek
   feta cheese

## method

**1** Heat the oil in a large, lidded skillet, add the onion, red bell pepper, and garlic, and fry for 5 minutes, until softened. Add the rice and cook for 2–3 minutes, stirring all the time, until the grains look transparent.

**2** Add the stock, bay leaf, salt, and pepper. Bring to a boil, cover the skillet with a tightly fitting lid, and simmer for about 15 minutes, until the rice is tender and the liquid has been absorbed. Do not stir during cooking. When cooked, very gently stir in the shrimp.

**3** Remove the lid, cover the skillet with a clean dish towel, replace the lid, and let stand in a warm place for 10 minutes to dry out. Stir with a fork to separate the grains and serve garnished with whole shrimp, lemon wedges, and black olives. Accompany with kefalotiri or pecorino cheese for sprinkling on top and a bowl of feta cubes.

# jamaican rice & peas

## ingredients

**SERVES 6–8**

1 lb/450 g/2 cups dried
  black-eyed peas, soaked
  in cold water overnight
2 tbsp vegetable oil
1 large onion, chopped
2–3 garlic cloves, chopped
2 fresh red chiles, seeded
  and chopped
1 lb/450 g/2 cups long-grain
  white rice
14 fl oz/400 ml canned
  coconut milk
$3/4$ tsp dried thyme
salt

### tomato salsa

4 tomatoes, seeded and cut
  into small pieces
1 red onion, finely chopped
4 tbsp chopped fresh cilantro
2 garlic cloves, finely chopped
1–2 fresh jalapeño chiles,
  seeded and thinly sliced
1–2 tbsp extra-virgin olive oil
1 tbsp fresh lime juice
1 tsp light brown sugar
salt and pepper

### to garnish

slices of lime
fresh cilantro leaves
fresh bird's eye chiles

## method

**1** Drain the soaked peas, rinse, and place in a large pan. Cover generously with cold water and bring to a boil over high heat, skimming off any foam. Boil vigorously for about 10 minutes (to remove any toxins), drain, rinse, and drain again. Return to the pan, cover with cold water again and bring to a boil over high heat. Reduce the heat to medium–low and let simmer, partially covered, for about $1^1/4$–$1^1/2$ hours or until tender. Drain, reserving the cooking liquid.

**2** Heat the oil in another pan. Add the onion and cook for about 2 minutes until softened. Stir in the garlic and chiles and cook for an additional 1 minute. Add the rice and stir until well coated.

**3** Stir in the coconut milk, thyme, and about 1 teaspoon salt. Add the cooked peas and 16 fl oz/450 ml of the reserved cooking liquid to cover; add more liquid if necessary. Bring the mixture to a boil, then reduce the heat to low, cover tightly, and cook for 20–25 minutes.

**4** Meanwhile, make the tomato salsa: combine all the ingredients in a bowl and let stand, loosely covered, at room temperature.

**5** Remove the rice from the heat and stand, covered, for 5 minutes, then fork into a serving bowl. Serve hot with the salsa on individual plates garnished with lime slices, fresh cilantro leaves, and bird's eye chiles.

# cashew nut paella

## ingredients

### SERVES 4–6

1 tbsp butter

2 tbsp olive oil

1 red onion, chopped

9 oz/250 g/³/₄ cup medium-
grain paella rice

1 tsp turmeric

1 tsp ground cumin

¹/₂ tsp chili powder

3 garlic cloves, crushed

1 fresh green chile, sliced

1 green bell pepper, seeded
and diced

1 red bell pepper, seeded and
diced

2³/₄ oz/75 g baby corn,
halved lengthwise

2 tbsp pitted black olives

1 large tomato, seeded
and diced

16 fl oz/450 ml/2 cups
vegetable stock

generous ¹/₂ cup unsalted
cashew nuts

2 oz/55 g/scant ¹/₂ cup
frozen peas

salt and pepper

2 tbsp chopped fresh parsley,
plus extra sprigs to garnish

pinch of cayenne pepper

## method

**1** Melt the butter with the oil in a paella pan or wide, shallow skillet and cook the onion over medium heat, stirring, for 2–3 minutes, or until softened.

**2** Add the rice, turmeric, cumin, chili powder, garlic, chile, bell peppers, baby corn, olives, and tomato and cook, stirring constantly, for 1–2 minutes. Pour in the stock and bring to a boil. Reduce the heat and cook, stirring frequently, for 20 minutes.

**3** Add the nuts and peas and cook, stirring occasionally, for 5 minutes. Season to taste with salt and pepper and sprinkle with the chopped parsley and cayenne pepper. Transfer to warmed serving plates, then garnish with parsley sprigs and serve immediately.

# basic basil risotto

## ingredients

SERVES 4

1 tbsp olive oil

3 tbsp butter

1 small onion, finely chopped

10 fresh basil leaves,
    chopped or shredded,
    plus extra whole leaves
    to garnish

4 tomatoes, seeded and diced

4 oz/115 g green beans, cut
    into 1-inch/2.5-cm lengths
    and cooked

10 oz/280 g/1$^1$/$_2$ cups
    Arborio rice

2 pints/1.2 liters/5 cups
    simmering vegetable or
    chicken stock
    (see page 18)

salt and pepper

2 tbsp pine nuts

3 oz/85 g/$^3$/$_4$ cup freshly
    grated Parmesan or Grana
    Padano cheese

## method

**1** Heat the oil with 2 tablespoons of the butter in a deep pan over medium heat until the butter has melted. Stir in the onion, three-quarters of the basil, the tomatoes, and beans and cook gently for 2–3 minutes for the flavors to blend. Reduce the heat, add the rice, and mix to coat in oil and butter. Cook, stirring constantly, for 2–3 minutes, or until the grains are translucent.

**2** Gradually add the hot stock, a ladleful at a time. Stir constantly and add more liquid as the rice absorbs each addition. Increase the heat to medium so that the liquid bubbles. Cook for 20 minutes, or until all the liquid is absorbed and the rice is creamy. Season to taste.

**3** While the risotto is cooking, heat a skillet over high heat. Add the pine nuts and dry-fry for 1–2 minutes, or until just starting to brown. Be careful not to let them burn.

**4** Remove the risotto from the heat and add the remaining butter. Carefully fold in the remaining chopped basil. Mix well, then stir in the Parmesan until it melts.

**5** Divide the risotto between 4 warmed plates and garnish with whole basil leaves and the pine nuts before serving.

# sunshine risotto

## ingredients

**SERVES 6**

about 12 sun-dried tomatoes

2 tbsp olive oil

1 large onion,
   finely chopped

4–6 garlic cloves,
   finely chopped

14 oz/400 g/generous
   1³/4 cups Arborio rice

2³/4 pints/1.5 liters/scant
   6¹/2 cups simmering
   chicken or vegetable stock
   (see page 18)

2 tbsp chopped fresh
   flat-leaf parsley

1 cup freshly grated aged
   romano cheese

extra-virgin olive oil,
   for drizzling

## method

**1** Place the sun-dried tomatoes in a heatproof bowl and pour over enough boiling water to cover. Set aside to soak for 30 minutes, or until soft and supple. Drain and pat dry with paper towels, then shred thinly and set aside.

**2** Heat the olive oil in a deep pan over medium heat. Add the onion and cook, stirring occasionally, for 2 minutes, or until starting to soften. Add the garlic and cook for an additional 15 seconds. Reduce the heat, add the rice, and mix to coat in oil. Cook, stirring constantly, for 2–3 minutes, or until the grains are translucent.

**3** Gradually add the hot stock, a ladleful at a time. Stir constantly and add more liquid as the rice absorbs each addition. Increase the heat to medium so that the liquid bubbles. After about 15 minutes, stir in the sun-dried tomatoes. Continue adding the stock, stirring constantly, until the risotto has been cooking for 20 minutes, or until all the liquid is absorbed and the rice is creamy.

**4** Remove the pan from the heat and stir in the chopped parsley and half the romano cheese. Spoon the risotto onto 6 warmed plates. Drizzle with extra-virgin olive oil and sprinkle the remaining romano cheese on top. Serve at once.

# lemon & rosemary risotto

## ingredients

**SERVES 4**

2 lemons

1 tbsp olive oil

3 tbsp butter

1 small onion,
  finely chopped

1 tbsp finely chopped fresh
  rosemary

10 oz/280 g/1$^1$/$_2$ cups
  Arborio rice

2 pints/1.2 liters/5 cups
  simmering vegetable or
  chicken stock
  (see page 18)

salt and pepper

3 oz/85 g/$^3$/$_4$ cup freshly grated
  Parmesan or
  Grana Padano cheese

## method

**1** Grate the lemon rinds and set aside. Squeeze the juice from the lemons into a small pan and place over medium heat until just about to boil.

**2** Heat the oil with 2 tablespoons of the butter in a deep pan over medium heat until the butter has melted. Stir in the onion and half the rosemary and cook gently, stirring occasionally, for 5 minutes, or until the onion is soft and translucent. Do not brown. Reduce the heat, add the rice, and mix to coat in oil and butter. Cook, stirring constantly, for 2–3 minutes, or until the grains are translucent.

**3** Gradually add the hot stock, a ladleful at a time, alternating with the lemon juice. Stir constantly and add more liquid as the rice absorbs each addition. Increase the heat to medium so that the liquid bubbles. Cook for 20 minutes, or until all the liquid is absorbed and the rice is creamy. Season to taste with salt and pepper.

**4** Remove the risotto from the heat and add the remaining butter and rosemary. Mix well, then stir in the Parmesan until it melts. Spoon the risotto onto individual plates and sprinkle with the grated lemon rind. Season and serve.

# minted green risotto

## ingredients

SERVES 6

2 tbsp butter

8 oz/225 g/generous
   $1\frac{1}{2}$ cups peas, thawed
   if frozen

9 oz/225 g/5$\frac{5}{8}$ cups fresh
   young spinach leaves,
   washed and drained

1 bunch of fresh mint, leaves
   stripped from stalks

2 tbsp chopped fresh basil

2 tbsp chopped fresh oregano

pinch of freshly grated nutmeg

4 tbsp mascarpone cheese or
   heavy cream

2 tbsp vegetable oil

1 onion, finely chopped

2 celery stalks, including
   leaves, finely chopped

2 garlic cloves, finely
   chopped

$\frac{1}{2}$ tsp dried thyme

$10\frac{1}{2}$ oz/300 g/scant
   $1\frac{1}{2}$ cups Arborio rice

2 fl oz/50 ml/$\frac{1}{4}$ cup dry
   white vermouth

$1\frac{3}{4}$ pints/1 liter/4 cups
   simmering chicken or
   vegetable stock
   (see page 18)

3 oz/85 g/$\frac{3}{4}$ cup freshly
   grated Parmesan cheese

## method

**1** Heat half the butter in a deep skillet over medium–high heat until sizzling. Add the peas, spinach, mint leaves, basil, and oregano and season with the nutmeg. Cook, stirring frequently, for 3 minutes, or until the spinach leaves and mint leaves are wilted. Let cool slightly, then process in a food processor for 15 seconds. Add the mascarpone (or cream) and process again for 1 minute. Transfer to a bowl and set aside.

**2** Heat the oil and remaining butter in a large, heavy-bottom pan over medium heat. Add the onion, celery, garlic, and thyme and cook, stirring occasionally, for 2 minutes, or until the vegetables are softened. Reduce the heat, add the rice, and mix to coat in oil and butter. Cook, stirring constantly, for 2–3 minutes, or until the grains are translucent. Add the vermouth and cook, stirring constantly, until it has reduced.

**3** Gradually add the hot stock, a ladleful at a time. Stir constantly and add more liquid as the rice absorbs each addition. Increase the heat to medium so that the liquid bubbles. Cook for 20 minutes, or until the liquid is absorbed and the rice is creamy.

**4** Stir in the spinach-mascarpone mixture and the Parmesan. Transfer to warmed plates and serve at once.

# rice & turkey salad

## ingredients

**SERVES 4**

1³/4 pints/1 liter/4 cups
   chicken stock
7 oz/200 g/scant 1 cup mixed
   long-grain and wild rice
2 tbsp corn oil
8 oz/225 g skinless, boneless
   turkey breast, trimmed of
   all visible fat and cut into
   thin strips
4 oz/115 g/2 cups snow peas
4 oz/115 g oyster mushrooms,
   torn into pieces
1 oz/25g/¹/4 cup shelled
   pistachio nuts,
   finely chopped
2 tbsp chopped fresh cilantro
1 tbsp snipped fresh
   garlic chives
salt and pepper
1 tbsp balsamic vinegar
fresh garlic chives, to garnish

## method

**1** Set aside 3 tablespoons of the chicken stock and bring the remainder to a boil in a large pan. Add the rice and cook for 30 minutes, or until tender. Drain and let cool slightly.

**2** Meanwhile, heat 1 tablespoon of the oil in a preheated wok or skillet. Stir-fry the turkey over medium heat for 3–4 minutes, or until cooked through. Using a slotted spoon, transfer the turkey to a dish. Add the snow peas and mushrooms to the wok and stir-fry for 1 minute. Add the reserved stock, bring to a boil, then reduce the heat, cover, and let simmer for 3–4 minutes. Transfer the vegetables to the dish and let cool slightly.

**3** Thoroughly mix the rice, turkey, snow peas, mushrooms, nuts, cilantro, and garlic chives together, then season to taste with salt and pepper. Drizzle with the remaining corn oil and the vinegar and garnish with fresh garlic chives. Serve warm.

# meat, poultry & seafood

Risotto is one of the best-loved dishes in Italy. It originated in northern Italy, where rice is grown—exactly where it was invented is a matter for debate, with several regions claiming the honor!

There is no denying that making a risotto demands all your attention—once the rice grains have been coated in a delicious mixture of butter and olive oil, you must stand over it stirring in the simmering stock a ladleful at a time. Far from being a chore, however, this is a brilliant way to unwind—just pour yourself a glass of wine and devote yourself to the task. When you sit down to eat the temptingly creamy risotto, with its plump grains bursting with flavor, you will have to agree that the effort was worthwhile.

With paella, however, the opposite applies. While you must keep a close eye on it so that it doesn't burn, you absolutely must not stir it while it is cooking. The trick here is to shake the pan once or twice, and if you are adding ingredients or a little extra stock, don't stir—shake! Paella is one of those marvelous dishes where you can throw in anything you have to hand—Poor Man's Paella is a great way to use up leftover meat or vegetables.

You'll find recipes from all cultures in this chapter, so you won't be short of main meal ideas for quite some time!

# egg-fried rice with seven-spice beef

## ingredients

**SERVES 4**

8 oz/225 g/generous 1 cup
    long-grain white rice

1 pint/600 ml/2$^{1}/_{2}$ cups water

12 oz/350 g beef tenderloin

2 tbsp dark soy sauce

2 tbsp tomato ketchup

1 tbsp seven-spice seasoning

2 tbsp peanut oil

1 onion, diced

3 small carrots, diced

3$^{1}/_{2}$ oz/100 g/1 cup frozen
    peas

2 eggs, beaten

2 tbsp cold water

## method

**1** Rinse the rice under cold running water, then drain thoroughly. Place the rice in a pan with the water, bring to a boil, cover, and let simmer for 12 minutes. Turn the cooked rice out onto a cookie sheet and let cool.

**2** Using a sharp knife, thinly slice the beef tenderloin and place in a large, shallow dish. Mix the soy sauce, tomato ketchup, and seven-spice seasoning. Spoon over the beef and toss well to coat.

**3** Heat the peanut oil in a preheated wok. Add the beef and stir-fry for 3–4 minutes. Add the onion, carrots, and peas and stir-fry for a further 2–3 minutes. Add the cooked rice to the wok and mix together.

**4** Beat the eggs with 2 tablespoons of cold water. Drizzle the egg mixture over the rice and stir-fry for 3–4 minutes, or until the rice is heated through and the egg has set. Transfer the rice and beef to a warm serving bowl and serve immediately.

# xinjiang rice pot with lamb

## ingredients

**SERVES 6–8**

2 tbsp vegetable or peanut oil

10$^1$/$_2$ oz/300 g lamb or mutton,
    cut into bite-size cubes

2 carrots, coarsely chopped

2 onions, coarsely chopped

1 tsp salt

1 tsp ground ginger

1 tsp Sichuan peppers, lightly
    roasted and lightly crushed

1lb/450 g/generous 2 cups
    short or medium-grain rice

1$^1$/$_2$ pints/850 ml/3$^3$/$_4$ cups
    water

## method

**1** In a large casserole, heat the oil and stir-fry
the meat for 1–2 minutes, or until the pieces
are sealed on all sides. Add the carrots and
onions and stir-fry until the vegetables are
beginning to soften. Add the salt, ginger, and
Sichuan peppers and mix well.

**2** Finally, add the rice and water and bring to a
boil. Cover the pan and cook over low heat for
30 minutes, or until the rice has absorbed all
the water. Serve alone or as part of a meal.

# hot pepper lamb in red wine risotto

## ingredients

SERVES 4

4 tbsp seasoned
    all-purpose flour
8 pieces neck of lamb or
    lamb chops
4 tbsp olive oil
1 green bell pepper, seeded
    and thinly sliced
1–2 fresh green chiies,
    seeded and thinly sliced
2 small onions, 1 thinly sliced
    and 1 finely chopped
2 garlic cloves, thinly sliced
2 tbsp torn fresh basil
4 fl oz/125 ml/$^{1}/_{2}$ cup
    red wine
4 tbsp red wine vinegar
8 cherry tomatoes
4 fl oz/125ml/$^{1}/_{2}$ cup water
3 tbsp butter
10 oz/280 g/1$^{1}/_{2}$ cups
    Arborio rice
2 pints/1.2 liters/5 cups
    simmering chicken stock
3 oz/85 g/$^{3}/_{4}$ cup freshly
    grated Parmesan or Grana
    Padano cheese
salt and pepper

## method

**1** Coat the lamb in the seasoned flour, shaking off any excess. Heat 3 tablespoons of the oil in a large ovenproof casserole over high heat. Add the lamb and cook until browned all over. Remove from the casserole and set aside.

**2** Toss the bell pepper, chiles, sliced onion, garlic, and basil in the oil left in the casserole until lightly browned. Add the wine and vinegar, bring to a boil, and cook for 3–4 minutes to reduce the liquid to 2 tablespoons. Add the tomatoes and the water, stir, and bring to a boil. Return the meat, cover, and cook over low heat for 30 minutes, or until the meat is tender, turning occasionally.

**3** To make the risotto, melt 2 tablespoons of the butter with the remaining oil in a pan over medium heat. Add the chopped onion and cook, stirring, until soft and starting to turn golden. Reduce the heat, add the rice, and mix to coat in oil and butter. Cook, stirring, for 2–3 minutes, or until translucent. Add the hot stock, a ladleful at a time, stirring constantly, until all the liquid is absorbed and the rice is creamy.  Season to taste.

**4** Remove the risotto from the heat and stir in the remaining butter and the Parmesan. Serve topped with bell peppers, tomatoes, and lamb.

# pork hash

## ingredients

SERVES 4

14 oz/400 g canned chopped
   tomatoes
1–1$1/4$ pints/600–700 ml/
   2$1/2$–3 cups beef stock
1 tbsp corn oil
1 lb/450 g fresh ground pork
1 large onion, chopped
1 red bell pepper, seeded and
   chopped
14 oz/400 g/2 cups
   long-grain rice
1 tbsp chili powder
1 lb/450 g fresh or frozen
   green beans
salt and pepper

## method

**1** Drain the tomatoes, reserving their juices, and reserve. Make the juices up to 1$1/2$ pints/ 850 ml/3$1/2$ cups with the stock and reserve.

**2** Heat the oil in a large, flameproof casserole. Add the pork, onion, and red bell pepper and cook over medium heat, stirring frequently, for 8–10 minutes, or until the onion is softened and the meat is broken up and golden brown. Add the rice and cook, stirring constantly, for 2 minutes.

**3** Add the tomatoes, stock mixture, chili powder, and beans to the casserole and season to taste with salt and pepper. Bring to a boil, then cover and transfer to a preheated oven, 350°F/180°C, to bake for 40 minutes. Serve immediately.

# spicy pork risotto

## ingredients

**SERVES 4**

1 thick slice white bread,
    crusts cut off and
    discarded
milk, for soaking
1 lb/450 g fresh ground pork
2 garlic cloves, minced
1 tbsp finely chopped onion
1 tsp black peppercorns,
    lightly crushed
pinch of salt
1 egg
corn oil, for pan-frying
14 oz/400 g canned chopped
    tomatoes
1 tbsp tomato paste
1 tsp dried oregano
1 tsp fennel seeds
pinch of sugar
3 tbsp butter
1 tbsp olive oil
1 small onion, finely chopped
10 oz/280 g/1$^1$/2 cups
    Arborio rice
5 fl oz/150 ml/$^2$/3 cup
    red wine
1$^3$/4 pints/1 liter/4 cups
    simmering beef stock
    (see page 18)
salt and pepper
fresh basil leaves, to garnish

## method

**1** Soak the bread in the milk for 5 minutes to soften. Drain and squeeze well to remove all the liquid. Mix the bread, pork, garlic, onion, crushed peppercorns, and salt together in a bowl. Add the egg and mix well. Form the meat mixture into balls. Heat the corn oil in a skillet over medium heat and brown the meatballs in batches. Drain, and set aside.

**2** Combine the tomatoes, tomato paste, oregano, fennel seeds, and sugar in a heavy-bottom pan. Add the meatballs. Bring the sauce to a boil over medium heat, then reduce the heat and let simmer for 30 minutes, or until the meat is thoroughly cooked.

**3** To make the risotto, melt 2 tablespoons of the butter with the olive oil in a deep pan over medium heat. Cook the onion, stirring, until soft and starting to turn golden. Reduce the heat, add the rice, and cook, stirring, for 2–3 minutes, or until the grains are translucent. Stir in the wine until it is absorbed, then stir in the hot stock, a ladleful at a time, stirring constantly, until all the liquid is absorbed and the rice is creamy. Season to taste.

**4** Lift out the cooked meatballs and add to the risotto. Remove the risotto from the heat and add the remaining butter. Mix well. Serve the risotto and meatballs on plates drizzled with tomato sauce and garnished with basil.

# five-spice crispy pork with egg-fried rice

## ingredients

**SERVES 4**

$9^1/_2$ oz/275 g/$1^1/_4$ cups
   long-grain white rice
1pint/600 ml/$2^1/_2$ cups
   cold water
salt and pepper
12 oz/350 g pork tenderloin
2 tsp Chinese five-spice
   powder
4 tbsp cornstarch
3 extra-large eggs
2 tbsp raw brown sugar
2 tbsp corn oil
1 onion, chopped
2 garlic cloves, minced
1 large carrot, diced
1 red bell pepper, seeded
   and diced
$3^1/_2$ oz/100 g/scant
   1 cup peas
1 tbsp butter

## method

**1** Rinse the rice in a strainer under cold running water. Place in a large pan, add the cold water and a pinch of salt. Bring to a boil, cover, then reduce the heat, and let simmer for about 9 minutes, or until all of the liquid has been absorbed and the rice is tender.

**2** Meanwhile, slice the pork into very thin, even-size pieces, using a sharp knife or meat cleaver. Set aside.

**3** Stir together the Chinese five-spice powder, cornstarch, 1 egg, and the raw brown sugar. Toss the pork in the mixture until coated.

**4** Heat the oil in a preheated wok or skillet. Add the pork and cook over high heat until the pork is cooked through and crispy. Remove the pork from the wok or skillet with a slotted spoon and keep warm.

**5** Add the onion, garlic, carrot, bell pepper, and peas to the wok or skillet and stir-fry for 5 minutes. Return the pork to the wok, together with the cooked rice, and stir-fry for 5 minutes.

**6** Heat the butter in a skillet. Beat the remaining eggs, add to the skillet, and cook until set. Turn out onto a clean board and slice thinly. Toss the strips of egg into the rice mixture and serve immediately.

# poor man's paella

## ingredients

**SERVES 4–6**

$^1/_2$ tsp saffron threads

2 tbsp hot water

4 tbsp olive oil

1 large carrot, blanched
    and minced

1 large onion, chopped

2 garlic cloves, crushed

1 tsp paprika

$^1/_4$ tsp cayenne pepper

8 oz/225 g tomatoes, peeled
    and cut into wedges

1 red bell pepper, halved
    and seeded, then broiled,
    peeled, and sliced

12 oz/350 g/1$^5/_8$ cups
    medium-grain paella rice

1 tbsp chopped fresh thyme

2$^1/_4$ pints/1.3 liters/5$^1/_2$ cups
    simmering chicken stock

6 oz/175 g cooked pork, cut
    into bite-size pieces

6 oz/175 g cooked chicken,
    cut into bite-size pieces

5$^1/_2$ oz/150 g green beans,
    blanched, or the same
    quantity of any leftover
    cooked vegetables

salt and pepper

3 hard-cooked eggs, cut
    lengthwise into fourths,
    to garnish

## method

**1** Put the saffron threads and water in a small bowl and let infuse for a few minutes.

**2** Heat half the oil in a paella pan and cook the carrot over medium heat, stirring, for 3 minutes. Add the onion and cook, stirring, until softened. Add half the garlic, the paprika, cayenne pepper, and saffron and its soaking liquid and cook, stirring, for 1 minute. Add the tomatoes and bell peppers and cook, stirring, for 2 minutes. Add the rice and thyme and cook, stirring, for 1 minute, to coat the rice. Add most of the hot stock and bring to a boil, then let simmer, uncovered, for 10 minutes. Do not stir during cooking, but shake the pan once or twice, and when adding ingredients.

**3** Meanwhile, heat the remaining oil in a separate skillet and cook the remaining garlic, pork, and chicken over high heat, stirring, for 5 minutes. The heat should be high enough for the meat to become hot and steamy. Transfer the mixture to the paella pan, then add the beans and season to taste. Cook for 10–15 minutes, or until the rice is cooked, adding a little more stock if necessary.

**4** When all the liquid has been absorbed and you detect a faint toasty aroma coming from the rice, remove from the heat. Cover with foil and let stand for 5 minutes. Garnish with the egg fourths and serve.

# sausage & pepper risotto

## ingredients

**SERVES 4**

8 sausages, sweet and/
   or spicy
1 red bell pepper, seeded and
   cut into 8 pieces
1 green bell pepper, seeded
   and cut into 8 pieces
1 onion, thickly sliced
4 tbsp olive oil
3 tbsp butter
1 small onion, finely chopped
10 oz/280 g/generous
   $1^3/_8$ cups Arborio rice
5 fl oz/150 ml/$^2/_3$ cup
   red wine
$1^3/_4$ pints/1 liter/4 cups
   simmering beef stock
   (see page 18)
3 oz/85 g/$^3/_4$ cup freshly
   grated Parmesan or Grana
   Padano cheese
salt and pepper
fresh rosemary sprigs,
   to garnish

## method

**1** Place the sausages in an ovenproof dish. Scatter the bell peppers and sliced onion around the sausages and sprinkle with 3 tablespoons of the olive oil. Cook the sausages and vegetables in a preheated oven, 375°F/190°C, for 20–30 minutes, turning occasionally.

**2** Heat the remaining oil with 2 tablespoons of the butter in a deep pan over medium heat until the butter has melted. Add the chopped onion and cook, stirring occasionally, for 5 minutes, or until soft and starting to turn golden. Do not brown.

**3** Reduce the heat, add the rice, and mix to coat in oil and butter. Cook, stirring constantly, for 2–3 minutes, or until the grains are translucent. Add the wine and cook, stirring constantly, for 1 minute until reduced.

**4** Add the hot stock, a ladleful at a time. Stir constantly and add more liquid as the rice absorbs each addition. Increase the heat to medium so that the liquid bubbles. Cook for 20 minutes, or until all the liquid is absorbed and the rice is creamy. Season to taste.

**5** Remove the risotto from the heat and add the remaining butter. Mix well, then stir in the Parmesan until it melts. Serve the risotto at once, topped with the bell peppers, onions and two sausages per person, and garnished with rosemary sprigs.

# sausage & rosemary risotto

## ingredients

### SERVES 4–6

2 long fresh rosemary sprigs,
plus extra to garnish

2 tbsp olive oil

2 oz/55 g butter

1 large onion, finely chopped

1 celery stalk, finely chopped

2 garlic cloves, finely chopped

$1/2$ tsp dried thyme leaves

1 lb/450 g pork sausages,
such as luganega or
Cumberland, cut into
$1/2$-inch/1-cm pieces

12 oz/350 g/generous
$1^1/2$ cups Arborio rice

4 fl oz/125 ml/$1/2$ cup
fruity red wine

$2^1/4$ pints/1.3 liters/$5^1/2$ cups
simmering chicken stock
(see page 18)

salt and pepper

3 oz/85 g/$3/4$ cup freshly
grated Parmesan cheese

## method

**1** Strip the long thin leaves from the rosemary sprigs and chop finely, then set aside.

**2** Heat the oil and half the butter in a deep pan over medium heat. Add the onion and celery and cook, stirring occasionally, for 2 minutes. Stir in the garlic, thyme, sausage, and rosemary. Cook, stirring frequently, for 5 minutes, or until the sausage starts to brown. Transfer the sausage to a plate. Reduce the heat, add the rice, and mix to coat in oil and butter. Cook, stirring constantly, for 2–3 minutes, or until the grains are translucent. Add the wine and cook, stirring constantly, for 1 minute until reduced.

**3** Gradually add the hot stock, a ladleful at a time. Stir constantly and add more liquid as the rice absorbs each addition. Increase the heat to medium so that the liquid bubbles. Cook for 20 minutes, or until all the liquid is absorbed and the rice is creamy. Toward the end of cooking, return the sausage pieces to the risotto and heat through. Season to taste with salt and pepper.

**4** Remove the risotto from the heat and add the remaining butter. Mix well, then melt in the Parmesan. Serve the risotto on warmed plates, garnished with rosemary sprigs.

# chorizo & ham paella

## ingredients

### SERVES 4–6

$^1/_2$ tsp saffron threads

2 tbsp hot water

3 tbsp olive oil

6 oz/175 g Spanish chorizo
   sausage, casing removed,
   cut into $^1/_2$-inch/1-cm slices

6 oz/175 g serrano ham, diced
   (if unavailable, use
   prosciutto)

1 large onion, chopped

2 garlic cloves, crushed

1 tsp paprika

$^1/_4$ tsp cayenne pepper

8 oz/225 g tomatoes, peeled
   and cut into wedges

1 red bell pepper, halved
   and seeded, then broiled,
   peeled, and sliced

12oz/350 g/1$^5/_8$ cups
   medium-grain paella rice

1 tbsp chopped fresh thyme

3 fl oz/125 ml/generous
   $^1/_3$ cup white wine

2 pints/1.2 liters/5 cups
   simmering beef or chicken
   stock or water

salt and pepper

1 tbsp chopped fresh parsley,
   to garnish

1 lemon, cut into wedges,
   to serve

## method

**1** Put the saffron threads and water in a small bowl and let infuse for a few minutes.

**2** Heat 2 tablespoons of the oil in a paella pan and cook the chorizo and ham over medium heat, stirring, for 5 minutes. Transfer to a bowl and set aside. Heat the remaining oil in the pan and cook the onion, stirring, until softened. Add the garlic, paprika, cayenne pepper, and saffron and its soaking liquid and cook, stirring constantly, for 1 minute. Add the tomato wedges and red bell pepper slices and cook, stirring, for an additional 2 minutes.

**3** Add the rice and thyme and cook, stirring, for 1 minute to coat the rice. Pour in the wine and most of the hot stock and bring to a boil, then let simmer, uncovered, for 10 minutes. Do not stir during cooking, but shake the pan once or twice and when adding ingredients. Season to taste and cook for 10 minutes, or until the rice is almost cooked. If the liquid is absorbed too quickly, pour in a little more hot stock. Return the chorizo and ham and any accumulated juices to the pan. Cook for 2 minutes.

**4** When all the liquid has been absorbed and you detect a faint toasty aroma coming from the rice, remove from the heat. Cover the pan with foil and let stand for 5 minutes. Garnish with parsley and serve with lemon wedges.

# sausage & bell pepper risotto

## ingredients

**SERVES 4**

2 tbsp peanut oil

1 onion, sliced

2 garlic cloves, minced

1 tsp Chinese five-spice
    powder

8 oz/225 g Chinese sausage,
    sliced

3 small carrots, diced

1 green bell pepper, seeded
    and diced

$9^1/_2$ oz/275 g/$1^1/_3$ cups
    Arborio rice

$1^1/_2$ pints/850 ml/$3^1/_2$ cups
    vegetable or chicken stock

6 fresh chives

## method

**1** Heat the peanut oil in a large preheated skillet, swirling it over the bottom. Add the onion slices, minced garlic, and Chinese five-spice powder and stir-fry for 1 minute. Add the Chinese sausage, carrots, and green bell pepper and stir to mix. Stir in the rice and cook for 1 minute.

**2** Gradually add the vegetable or chicken stock, a little at a time, stirring constantly, until the liquid has been completely absorbed and the rice grains are tender.

**3** Snip the chives with a pair of clean kitchen scissors and stir into the wok with the last of the stock. Transfer the Chinese risotto to warmed individual serving bowls and serve immediately.

# paella primavera

## ingredients

**SERVES 4–6**

$^1/_2$ tsp saffron threads

2 tbsp hot water

3 tbsp olive oil

6 oz/175 g serrano ham, diced

1 large carrot, diced

$5^1/_2$ oz/150 g white mushrooms

4 large scallions, diced

2 garlic cloves, crushed

1 tsp paprika

$^1/_4$ tsp cayenne pepper

8 oz/225 g tomatoes, peeled and cut into wedges

1 red bell pepper, halved and seeded, then broiled, peeled, and sliced

1 green bell pepper, halved and seeded, then broiled, peeled, and sliced

12 oz/350 g/$1^5/_8$ cups medium-grain paella rice

2 tbsp chopped mixed fresh herbs, plus extra to garnish

$3^1/_2$ fl oz/100 ml/$^1/_3$ cup white wine

2 pints/1.2 liters/5 cups simmering chicken stock

2 oz/55 g/$^3/_8$ cup shelled peas

$3^1/_2$ oz/100 g fresh asparagus spears, blanched

salt and pepper

lemon wedges, to serve

## method

**1** Put the saffron threads and water in a small bowl and let infuse for a few minutes.

**2** Heat 2 tablespoons of the oil in a paella pan and cook the ham over medium heat, stirring, for 5 minutes. Transfer to a bowl. Heat the remaining oil in the pan and cook the carrot, stirring, for 3 minutes. Add the mushrooms and cook, stirring, for 2 minutes. Add the scallions, garlic, paprika, cayenne pepper, and saffron and its soaking liquid and cook, stirring, for 1 minute. Add the tomatoes and bell peppers and cook, stirring, for 2 minutes.

**3** Add the rice and herbs and cook, stirring, for 1 minute, to coat the rice. Pour in the wine and most of the hot stock and bring to a boil, then let simmer, uncovered, for 10 minutes. Do not stir during cooking, but shake the pan once or twice and when adding ingredients. Add the peas and season to taste. Cook for 10 minutes, or until the rice is almost cooked, adding a little more stock if necessary. Return the ham and any juices to the pan. Arrange the asparagus around the paella in a wheel pattern and cook for 2 minutes.

**4** When all the liquid has been absorbed and you detect a faint toasty aroma coming from the rice, remove from the heat. Cover with foil and let stand for 5 minutes. Sprinkle over chopped herbs to garnish and serve with lemon wedges.

# oven-baked risotto with mushrooms

## ingredients

**SERVES 4**

4 tbsp olive oil

14 oz/400 g portobello
   mushrooms, thickly sliced

4 oz/115 g pancetta or thick-cut
   smoked bacon, diced

1 large onion, finely chopped

2 garlic cloves, finely
   chopped

12 oz/350 g/1$^3$/$_4$ cups
   Arborio rice

2$^1$/$_4$ pints/1.3 liters/5$^1$/$_2$ cups
   simmering chicken or
   vegetable stock
   (see page 18)

2 tbsp chopped fresh tarragon
   or flat-leaf parsley

salt and pepper

3 oz/85 g/$^3$/$_4$ cup freshly
   grated Parmesan cheese,
   plus extra for sprinkling

## method

**1** Heat half the oil in a large, heavy-bottom skillet over high heat. Add the mushrooms and stir-fry for 2–3 minutes until golden and tender-crisp. Transfer to a plate. Add the pancetta to the skillet and cook, stirring, for 2 minutes, or until crisp and golden. Remove with a slotted spoon and add to the mushrooms on the plate.

**2** Heat the remaining oil in a large pan over medium heat. Add the onion and cook, stirring occasionally, for 2 minutes. Add the garlic and cook for 1 minute. Reduce the heat, add the rice, and mix to coat in oil. Cook, stirring constantly, for 2–3 minutes, or until the grains are translucent.

**3** Gradually stir the hot stock into the rice, then add the mushroom and pancetta mixture and the tarragon. Season to taste with salt and pepper. Bring to a boil. Remove the pan from the heat and transfer the mixture to an ovenproof dish.

**4** Cover the dish and bake in a preheated oven, 350°F/180°C, for 20 minutes, or until the rice is almost tender and most of the liquid is absorbed. Uncover and stir in the Parmesan. Continue to bake for an additional 15 minutes until the rice is creamy. Serve at once with extra Parmesan for sprinkling.

# chicken, mushroom & cashew risotto

## ingredients

**SERVES 4**

2 oz/55 g butter

1 onion, chopped

9 oz/250 g skinless, boneless chicken breasts, diced

12 oz/350 g/1$^3$/$_4$ cups Arborio rice

2$^1$/$_4$ pints/1.3 liters/generous 5$^1$/$_2$ cups simmering chicken stock (see page 18)

1 tsp ground turmeric

5 fl oz/350 g/$^2$/$_3$ cup white wine

2$^3$/$_4$ oz/75 g crimini mushrooms, sliced

1$^3$/$_4$ oz/50 g/scant $^1$/$_3$ cup cashews, halved

salt and pepper

### to garnish

wild arugula

fresh Parmesan cheese shavings

fresh basil leaves

## method

**1** Melt the butter in a large pan over medium heat. Add the onion and cook, stirring occasionally, for 5 minutes, or until softened. Add the chicken and cook, stirring frequently, for an additional 5 minutes. Reduce the heat, add the rice, and mix to coat in butter. Cook, stirring constantly, for 2–3 minutes, or until the grains are translucent. Stir in the turmeric, then add the wine. Cook, stirring constantly, for 1 minute until reduced.

**2** Gradually add the hot stock, a ladleful at a time. Stir constantly and add more liquid as the rice absorbs each addition. Increase the heat to medium so that the liquid bubbles. Cook for 20 minutes, or until all the liquid is absorbed and the rice is creamy. About 3 minutes before the end of the cooking time, stir in the mushrooms and cashews. Season to taste with salt and pepper.

**3** Arrange the arugula leaves on 4 individual serving plates. Remove the risotto from the heat and spoon it over the arugula. Sprinkle over the Parmesan shavings and basil leaves and serve.

# chicken risotto with saffron

## ingredients

**SERVES 4**

4$^1$/$_2$ oz/125 g butter

2 lb/900 g skinless, boneless
chicken breasts,
thinly sliced

1 large onion, chopped

1 lb 2 oz/500 g/2$^1$/$_2$ cups
Arborio rice

5 fl oz/150 ml/$^2$/$_3$ cup
white wine

1 tsp crumbled saffron threads

2$^1$/$_4$ pints/1.3 liters/generous
5$^1$/$_2$ cups simmering
chicken stock
(see page 18)

salt and pepper

2 oz/55g/$^1$/$_2$ cup freshly grated
Parmesan cheese

## method

**1** Heat 2 oz/55 g of the butter in a deep pan, and add the chicken and onion and cook, stirring frequently, for 8 minutes, or until golden brown. Add the rice and mix to coat in the butter. Cook, stirring constantly for 2–3 minutes, or until the grains are translucent. Add the wine and cook, stirring constantly, for 1 minute until reduced.

**2** Mix the saffron with 4 tablespoons of the hot stock. Add the liquid to the rice and cook, stirring constantly, until it is absorbed. Gradually add the remaining hot stock, a ladleful at a time. Stir constantly and add more liquid as the rice absorbs each addition. Cook for 20 minutes, or until all the liquid is absorbed and the rice is creamy. Season to taste.

**3** Remove the risotto from the heat and add the remaining butter. Mix well, then stir in the Parmesan until it melts. Spoon the risotto onto warmed plates and serve at once.

# risotto with chargrilled chicken breast

## ingredients

**SERVES 4**

4 boneless chicken breasts,
  about 4 oz/115 g each
salt and pepper
grated rind and juice of
  1 lemon
5 tbsp olive oil
1 garlic clove, crushed
8 fresh thyme sprigs,
  finely chopped
3 tbsp butter
1 small onion, finely chopped
10 oz/280 g/1 1/2 cups
  Arborio rice
5 fl oz/150 ml/2/3 cup
  dry white wine
1 3/4 pints/1 liter/4 cups
  simmering chicken stock
  (see page 18)
3 oz/85 g/3/4 cup freshly grated
  Parmesan or
  Grana Padano cheese

to garnish
lemon wedges
fresh thyme sprigs

## method

**1** Place the chicken breasts in a shallow, nonmetallic dish and season. Mix together the lemon rind and juice, 4 tablespoons of the olive oil, the garlic, and thyme. Spoon over the chicken and rub in. Cover with plastic wrap and let marinate in the refrigerator for 4–6 hours, then return to room temperature.

**2** Preheat a grill pan over high heat. Cook the chicken, skin-side down, for 10 minutes, or until the skin is crisp and starting to brown. Turn over and brown the underside. Reduce the heat and cook for 10–15 minutes, or until the juices run clear. Let rest on a carving board for 5 minutes, then cut into thick slices.

**3** Meanwhile, melt 2 tablespoons of the butter with the remaining oil in a pan over medium heat. Cook the onion, stirring occasionally, until soft and starting to turn golden. Reduce the heat, stir in the rice, and cook, stirring, for 2–3 minutes, until translucent. Add the wine and cook, stirring, for 1 minute until reduced. Add the hot stock, a ladleful at a time, stirring constantly, until all the liquid is absorbed and the rice is creamy. Season to taste. Remove from the heat and stir in the remaining butter, then melt in the Parmesan. Serve at once, topped with the chicken slices and garnished with lemon wedges and thyme sprigs.

# greek chicken & rice

## ingredients

**SERVES 4**

8 chicken thighs

2 tbsp corn oil

1 onion, chopped

2 garlic cloves, finely chopped

6 oz/175 g/scant 1 cup
  long-grain rice

8 fl oz/225 ml/scant 1 cup
  chicken stock

1 lb 12 oz/800 g canned
  chopped tomatoes

1 tbsp chopped fresh thyme

2 tbsp chopped fresh oregano

12 black olives, pitted and
  chopped

2 oz/55 g feta cheese,
  crumbled

fresh oregano sprigs,
  to garnish

## method

**1** Remove the skin from the chicken. Heat the oil in a flameproof casserole. Add the chicken, in batches, if necessary, and cook over medium heat, turning occasionally, for 8–10 minutes, or until golden. Transfer to a plate with a perforated spoon.

**2** Add the onion, garlic, long-grain rice, and a scant ¼ cup of the stock to the casserole and cook, stirring, for 5 minutes, or until the onion is softened. Pour in the remaining stock and add the tomatoes and their juices and the herbs.

**3** Return the chicken thighs to the casserole, pushing them down into the rice. Bring to a boil, then reduce the heat, cover, and simmer for 25–30 minutes, or until the chicken is cooked through and tender. Stir in the olives and sprinkle the cheese on top. Garnish with oregano sprigs and serve immediately.

# chicken with vegetables & cilantro rice

## ingredients

SERVES 4

2 tbsp vegetable or peanut oil

1 red onion, chopped

2 garlic cloves, chopped

1-inch piece fresh gingerroot, peeled and chopped

2 skinless, boneless chicken breasts, cut into strips

4 oz/115 g white mushrooms

14 oz/400 g canned coconut milk

2 oz/50 g sugar snap peas, trimmed and halved lengthwise

2 tbsp soy sauce

1 tbsp fish sauce

### rice

1 tbsp vegetable or peanut oil

1 red onion, sliced

12 oz/350 g/3 cups rice, cooked and cooled

8 oz/250 g bok choy, torn into large pieces

handful of fresh cilantro, chopped

2 tbsp Thai soy sauce

## method

**1** Heat the oil in a wok or large skillet and sauté the onion, garlic, and ginger together for 1–2 minutes.

**2** Add the chicken and mushrooms and cook over high heat until browned. Add the coconut milk, sugar snap peas, soy sauce, and fish sauce, and bring to a boil. Let simmer gently for 4–5 minutes until tender.

**3** Heat the oil for the rice in a separate wok or large skillet and cook the onion until softened but not browned. Add the cooked rice, bok choy, and fresh cilantro, and heat gently until the leaves have wilted and the rice is hot. Sprinkle over the soy sauce and serve immediately with the chicken.

# chinese chicken rice

## ingredients

**SERVES 4**

12 oz/350 g/1³/₄ cups
   long-grain white rice
1 tsp ground turmeric
salt
2 tbsp corn oil
12 oz/350 g skinless, boneless
   chicken thighs, sliced
1 red bell pepper, seeded
   and sliced
1 green bell pepper, seeded
   and sliced
1 fresh green chile, seeded
   and finely chopped
1 carrot, grated coarsely
5¹/₂ oz/150 g/1¹/₂ cups
   bean sprouts
6 scallions, sliced, plus extra
   to garnish
2 tbsp light soy sauce

## method

**1** Place the rice and turmeric in a large pan of lightly salted water and cook until the grains of rice are just tender, about 10 minutes. Drain the rice thoroughly and press out any excess water with paper towels.

**2** Heat the corn oil in a large preheated skillet. Add the strips of chicken and stir-fry over high heat until just starting to turn a golden color. Add the sliced bell peppers and green chile to the wok and stir-fry for 2–3 minutes.

**3** Add the cooked rice to the wok, a little at a time, tossing well after each addition until well mixed and the grains of rice are separated. Add the carrot, bean sprouts, and scallions to the wok and stir-fry for an additional 2 minutes. Drizzle with the soy sauce and toss to mix.

**4** Transfer the Chinese chicken rice to a warmed serving dish, garnish with extra scallions, if you like, and serve immediately.

# chicken jambalaya

## ingredients

**SERVES 4**

14 oz/400 g skinless, boneless
   chicken breast, diced
1 red onion, diced
1 garlic clove, crushed
1 pint/600 ml/2$^1$/$_2$ cups
   chicken stock
14 oz/400 g canned chopped
   tomatoes in tomato juice
10 oz/280 g/generous
   1$^1$/$_2$ cups brown rice
1–2 tsp hot chili powder
$^1$/$_2$ tsp paprika
1 tsp dried oregano
1 red bell pepper, seeded
   and diced
1 yellow bell pepper, seeded
   and diced
3 oz/85 g/$^1$/$_2$ cup frozen
   corn kernels
3 oz/85 g/$^3$/$_4$ cup frozen peas
3 tbsp chopped fresh parsley
freshly ground black pepper
crisp green salad, to serve
   (optional)

## method

**1** Put the chicken, onion, garlic, stock, tomatoes, and rice in a large, heavy-bottom pan. Add the chili powder, paprika, and oregano and stir well. Bring to a boil, then reduce the heat, cover, and let simmer for 25 minutes.

**2** Add the red and yellow bell peppers, corn, and peas to the rice mixture and return to a boil. Reduce the heat, cover, and let simmer for an additional 10 minutes, or until the rice is just tender (brown rice retains a "nutty" texture when cooked) and most of the stock has been absorbed but is not completely dry.

**3** Stir in 2 tablespoons of the parsley and season to taste with pepper. Transfer the jambalaya to a warmed serving dish, garnish with the remaining parsley, and serve with a crisp green salad (optional).

# chicken basquaise

## ingredients

SERVES 4

1 chicken, about 3 lb/1.3 kg,
    cut into 8 pieces
2 tbsp all-purpose flour
salt and pepper
3 tbsp olive oil
1 Spanish onion, thickly
    sliced
2 red or yellow bell peppers,
    seeded and cut lengthwise
    into thick strips
2 garlic cloves, finely chopped
5 oz/140 g spicy chorizo
    sausage, peeled and cut
    into $1/2$-inch/1-cm pieces
1 tbsp tomato paste
7 oz/200 g/1 cup
    long-grain rice
16 fl oz/450 ml/2 cups
    chicken stock
1 tsp chile flakes
$1/2$ tsp dried thyme
4 oz/115 g Bayonne ham,
    diced
12 dry-cured black olives
2 tbsp chopped fresh
    flat-leaf parsley

## to garnish

lemon slices
fresh flat-leaf parsley sprigs

## method

**1** Pat the chicken pieces dry with paper towels. Place the flour in a large plastic bag, season with salt and pepper, and add the chicken pieces. Seal the bag and shake to coat the chicken.

**2** Heat 2 tablespoons of the oil in a flameproof casserole. Add the chicken and cook over medium–high heat, turning frequently, for 15 minutes, or until browned. Transfer to a plate and set aside.

**3** Heat the remaining oil in the casserole and add the onion and bell peppers. Reduce the heat to medium and stir-fry until the onions color and soften. Add the garlic, chorizo, and tomato paste and cook, stirring, for 3 minutes, then add the rice and cook, stirring to coat, for 2 minutes, or until translucent.

**4** Add the stock, chile flakes, and thyme, season to taste, and stir well. Bring to a boil. Return the chicken to the casserole, pressing it gently into the rice. Cover and cook over very low heat for 45 minutes, or until the chicken is cooked through and the rice is tender.

**5** Gently stir the ham, olives, and half the parsley into the rice mixture. Re-cover and heat through for an additional 5 minutes. Sprinkle with the remaining parsley. Serve garnished with lemon slices and parsley sprigs.

# chicken & shrimp paella

## ingredients

**SERVES 6–8**

$^1\!/_2$ tsp saffron threads

2 tbsp hot water

about 6 tbsp olive oil

6–8 unboned, skin-on chicken
thighs, excess fat removed

5 oz/140 g Spanish chorizo
sausage, casing removed,
cut into $^1\!/_4$-inch/5-mm slices

2 large onions, chopped

4 large garlic cloves, crushed

1 tsp mild or hot Spanish
paprika, to taste

13 oz/375 g/generous
$1^3\!/_4$ cups medium-grain
paella rice, rinsed under
cold water

$3^1\!/_2$ oz/100 g green beans,
chopped

3 oz/85 g/$^3\!/_4$ cup frozen peas

2 pints/1.2 liters/5 cups
chicken stock

16 live mussels, scrubbed and
debearded (discard any
that refuse to close)

16 raw shrimp, shelled and
deveined

salt and pepper

2 red bell peppers, broiled,
peeled, and sliced

$1^1\!/_4$ oz/35 g fresh parsley,
chopped, to garnish

## method

**1** Put the saffron threads and water in a small bowl and let infuse for a few minutes.

**2** Heat 3 tablespoons of the oil in a 12-inch/ 30-cm paella pan. Cook the chicken thighs over medium–high heat, turning frequently, for 5 minutes, or until golden and crispy. Transfer to a bowl. Add the chorizo to the pan and cook, stirring, for 1 minute, or until beginning to crisp. Add to the chicken.

**3** Heat another 3 tablespoons of the oil in the pan and cook the onions, stirring frequently, for 2 minutes, then add the garlic and paprika and cook, stirring, for 3 minutes, or until the onions are soft but not browned. Add the drained rice, beans, and peas and stir until coated in oil. Return the chicken and chorizo and any juices to the pan. Stir in the stock and the saffron with its soaking liquid, and season to taste. Bring to a boil, stirring constantly, then let simmer, uncovered and without stirring, for 15 minutes, or until the rice is almost tender and most of the liquid has been absorbed.

**4** Arrange the mussels, shrimp, and red bell pepper slices on top, then cover and let simmer, without stirring, for 5 minutes, or until the shrimp turn pink and the mussels open. Discard any mussels that remain closed. Serve immediately, sprinkled with the parsley.

# sunshine paella

## ingredients

**SERVES 4**

$^1/_2$ tsp saffron threads

2 tbsp hot water

$5^1/_2$ oz/150 g cod, rinsed

42 fl oz/1.25 liters/$5^1/_2$ cups
  simmering fish stock

12 large raw shrimp, shelled
  and deveined

7 oz/200 g live mussels,
  scrubbed and debearded

3 tbsp olive oil

$5^1/_2$ oz/150 g chicken breast,
  cut into bite-size chunks
  and seasoned to taste

1 large red onion, chopped

2 garlic cloves, chopped

$^1/_2$ tsp cayenne pepper

$^1/_2$ tsp paprika

8 oz/225 g tomatoes, peeled
  and cut into wedges

1 red bell pepper and
  1 yellow bell pepper,
  seeded and sliced

13 oz/375 g/$1^5/_8$ cups
  medium-grain paella rice

6 oz/175 g/scant 1 cup
  canned corn kernels,
  drained

3 hard-cooked eggs, cut into
  fourths lengthwise,
  to serve

salt and pepper

lemon wedges, to serve

## method

**1** Put the saffron threads and water in a bowl and let infuse. Cook the cod in the simmering stock for 5 minutes. Rinse under cold running water, drain, cut into chunks, and set aside in a bowl. Cook the shrimp in the stock for 2 minutes. Add to the cod. Discard any mussels with broken shells or that refuse to close when tapped. Add to the stock and cook until opened. Add to the bowl with the other seafood, discarding any that remain closed.

**2** Heat the oil in a paella pan over medium heat. Cook the chicken, stirring, for 5 minutes. Add the onion and cook, stirring, until softened. Add the garlic, cayenne pepper, paprika, and saffron and its soaking liquid and cook, stirring, for 1 minute. Add the tomatoes and bell peppers and cook, stirring, for 2 minutes.

**3** Add the rice and cook, stirring, for 1 minute. Add most of the stock, bring to a boil, then let simmer, uncovered, for 10 minutes. Do not stir during cooking, but shake the pan once or twice and when adding ingredients. Season, then cook for 10 minutes, or until the rice is almost cooked, adding more stock if necessary. Add the seafood and corn and cook for 3 minutes.

**4** When all the liquid has been absorbed and you detect a faint toasty aroma coming from the rice, remove from the heat. Cover with foil and let stand for 5 minutes. Serve topped with egg fourths and garnished with lemon wedges.

# risotto with sole & tomatoes

## ingredients

**SERVES 4**

3 tbsp butter

3 tbsp olive oil

1 small onion, finely chopped

10 oz/280 g/1½ cups
   Arborio rice

2 pints/1.2 liters/5 cups
   simmering fish or chicken
   stock (see page 18)

salt and pepper

1 lb/450 g tomatoes, peeled,
   seeded, and cut into strips

6 sun-dried tomatoes in olive
   oil, drained and thinly sliced

3 tbsp tomato paste

2 fl oz/50 ml/¼ cup red wine

1 lb/450 g sole or flounder
   fillets, skinned

4 oz/115 g/1 cup freshly
   grated Parmesan or Grana
   Padano cheese

2 tbsp finely chopped fresh
   cilantro, to garnish

## method

**1** Melt 2 tablespoons of the butter with 1 tablespoon of the oil in a deep pan over medium heat. Stir in the onion and cook, stirring occasionally, for 5 minutes, or until soft and starting to turn golden. Reduce the heat, add the rice, and mix to coat in oil and butter. Cook, stirring constantly, for 2–3 minutes, or until the grains are translucent. Add the hot stock, a ladleful at a time, stirring constantly, until all the liquid is absorbed and the rice is creamy. Season to taste.

**2** Meanwhile, heat the remaining oil in a large, heavy-bottom skillet. Add the fresh and dried tomatoes. Stir well and cook over medium heat for 10–15 minutes, or until soft and slushy. Stir in the tomato paste and wine. Bring to a boil, then reduce the heat until it is just simmering. Cut the fish into strips and gently stir into the sauce. Cook for 5 minutes, or until the fish flakes when checked with a fork. Most of the liquid should be absorbed, but if it isn't, remove the fish and then increase the heat to reduce the sauce.

**3** Remove the risotto from the heat when all the liquid has been absorbed and add the remaining butter. Mix well, then stir in the Parmesan until it melts. Place the risotto on serving plates and arrange the fish and sauce on top. Garnish with chopped fresh cilantro and serve at once.

# risotto with tuna & pine nuts

## ingredients

**SERVES 4**

3 tbsp butter

4 tbsp olive oil

1 small onion, finely chopped

10 oz/280 g/1$^1$/$_2$ cups
    Arborio rice

2 pints/1.2 liters/5 cups
    simmering fish or chicken
    stock (see page 18)

salt and pepper

8 oz/225 g tuna, canned
    and drained, or broiled
    fresh steaks

8–10 black olives, pitted
    and sliced

1 small pimiento, thinly sliced

1 tsp finely chopped
    fresh parsley

1 tsp finely chopped
    fresh marjoram

2 tbsp white wine vinegar

2 oz/55 g/$^3$/$_8$ cup pine nuts

1 garlic clove, chopped

8 oz/225 g fresh tomatoes,
    peeled, seeded, and diced

3 oz/85 g/$^3$/$_4$ cup Parmesan
    or Grana Padano cheese

## method

**1** Melt 2 tablespoons of the butter with 1 tablespoon of the oil in a deep pan over medium heat. Add the onion and cook, stirring occasionally, until soft and starting to turn golden. Reduce the heat, add the rice, and mix to coat in oil and butter. Cook, stirring constantly, until the grains are translucent. Add the hot stock, a ladleful at a time, stirring constantly, until all the liquid is absorbed and the rice is creamy. Season to taste.

**2** While the risotto is cooking, flake the tuna into a bowl and mix in the olives, pimiento, parsley, marjoram, and vinegar. Season to taste with salt and pepper.

**3** Heat the remaining oil in a small skillet over high heat. Add the pine nuts and garlic. Cook, stirring constantly, for 2 minutes, or until they just start to brown. Add the tomatoes and mix well. Continue cooking over medium heat for 3–4 minutes or until they are thoroughly warm. Pour the tomato mixture over the tuna mixture and mix. Fold into the risotto 5 minutes before the end of the cooking time.

**4** Remove the risotto from the heat when all the liquid has been absorbed and add the remaining butter. Mix well, then stir in the Parmesan until it melts. Serve at once.

# rice & tuna bell peppers

## ingredients

SERVES 4

2 oz/55 g/generous
   $1/4$ cup wild rice
2 oz/55 g/generous
   $1/4$ cup brown rice
4 assorted medium
   bell peppers
7 oz/200 g canned tuna in
   brine, drained and flaked
$11^1/2$ oz/325 g canned corn
   kernels (with no added
   sugar or salt), drained
$3^1/2$ oz/100 g sharp Cheddar
   cheese, grated
1 bunch of fresh basil leaves,
   shredded
salt and pepper
2 tbsp dry white bread crumbs
1 tbsp freshly grated
   Parmesan cheese
fresh basil leaves, to garnish
crisp salad greens, to serve

## method

**1** Preheat the broiler to medium. Place the wild rice and brown rice in separate pans, cover with water, and cook for 15 minutes, or according to the package instructions. Drain and set aside.

**2** Meanwhile, halve the bell peppers, remove the seeds and stalks and arrange the bell peppers on a broiler rack, cut-side down. Cook under the hot broiler for 5 minutes, turn over, and cook for 4–5 minutes.

**3** Transfer the rice to a large bowl and add the tuna and corn. Gently fold in the grated cheese. Stir the basil leaves into the rice mixture, and season to taste with salt and pepper.

**4** Divide the tuna and rice mixture into 8 equal portions, then pile one portion into each cooked bell pepper half. Mix the bread crumbs and Parmesan cheese together in a bowl and sprinkle over each bell pepper. Place the bell peppers under the preheated hot broiler and cook for 4–5 minutes, or until hot and golden brown. Transfer the peppers to a large serving plate, garnish with fresh basil leaves, and serve immediately with crisp salad greens.

# seafood paella with lemon & herbs

## ingredients

**SERVES 4–6**

$^1/_2$ tsp saffron threads

2 tbsp hot water

$5^1/_2$ oz/150 g cod fillet, skinned and rinsed under cold running water

42 fl oz/1.25 liters/$5^1/_2$ cups simmering fish stock

12 large raw shrimp, shelled and deveined

1 lb/450 g raw squid, cleaned and cut into rings or bite-size pieces (or use the same quantity of shelled scallops)

3 tbsp olive oil

1 large red onion, chopped

2 garlic cloves, crushed

1 small fresh red chile, seeded and minced

8 oz/225 g tomatoes, peeled and cut into wedges

13 oz/375 g/generous $1^1/_2$ cups medium-grain paella rice

1 tbsp chopped fresh parsley

2 tsp chopped fresh dill

salt and pepper

1 lemon, cut into halves, to serve

## method

**1** Put the saffron threads and water in a small bowl and let infuse for a few minutes.

**2** Add the cod to the pan of simmering stock and cook for 5 minutes, then transfer to a colander, rinse under cold running water and drain. Add the shrimp and squid to the stock and cook for 2 minutes. Cut the cod into chunks, then transfer with the other seafood to a bowl and set aside. Let the stock simmer.

**3** Heat the oil in a paella pan and stir the onion over medium heat until softened. Add the garlic, chile, and saffron and its soaking liquid and cook, stirring, for 1 minute. Add the tomato wedges and cook, stirring, for 2 minutes. Add the rice and herbs and cook, stirring, for 1 minute. Add most of the stock and bring to a boil. Let simmer, uncovered, for 10 minutes. Do not stir during cooking, but shake the pan once or twice and when adding ingredients. Season and cook for 10 minutes, until the rice is almost cooked. Add more stock if necessary. Add the seafood and cook for 2 minutes.

**4** When all the liquid has been absorbed and you detect a faint toasty aroma coming from the rice, remove from the heat immediately. Cover with foil and let stand for 5 minutes. Serve with the lemon halves.

# saffron & lemon risotto with scallops

## ingredients

**SERVES 4**

16 live scallops, shucked

juice of 1 lemon, plus extra
    for seasoning

3 tbsp butter

1 tbsp olive oil, plus extra for
    brushing

1 small onion, finely chopped

10 oz/280 g/1$1/2$ cups
    Arborio rice

2 pints/1.2 liters/5 cups
    simmering fish or
    vegetable stock
    (see page 18)

salt and pepper

1 tsp crumbled
    saffron threads

2 tbsp vegetable oil

4 oz/115 g/1 cup freshly
    grated Parmesan or Grana
    Padano cheese

## to garnish

1 lemon, cut into wedges

2 tsp grated lemon zest

## method

**1** Place the scallops in a nonmetallic bowl and mix with the lemon juice. Cover the bowl with plastic wrap and let chill for 15 minutes.

**2** Melt 2 tablespoons of the butter with the oil in a deep pan over medium heat. Add the onion and cook, stirring occasionally, until soft and starting to turn golden. Add the rice and mix to coat in oil and butter. Cook, stirring, until the grains are translucent. Dissolve the saffron in 4 tablespoons of hot stock and add to the rice. Gradually add the remaining stock a ladleful at a time, stirring constantly, until all the liquid is absorbed and the rice is creamy. Season to taste.

**2** When the risotto is nearly cooked, preheat a grill pan over high heat. Brush the scallops with oil and sear on the grill pan for 3–4 minutes on each side, depending on their thickness. Take care not to overcook or they will be rubbery.

**3** Remove the risotto from the heat and add the remaining butter. Mix well, then stir in the Parmesan until it melts. Season with lemon juice, adding just 1 teaspoon at a time and tasting as you go. Serve the risotto at once with the scallops and lemon wedges arranged on top, sprinkled with lemon zest.

# black risotto

## ingredients

**SERVES 6**

2–3 tbsp olive oil

1 lb/450 g cleaned raw squid
   or cuttlefish, cut crosswise
   into thin strips, rinsed and
   patted dry

2 tbsp lemon juice

2 tbsp butter

3–4 garlic cloves,
   finely chopped

1 tsp crushed dried chili,
   or to taste

12 oz/350 g/1$^3$/$_4$ cups
   Arborio rice

1$^3$/$_4$ pints/1 liter/4 cups
   simmering fish or chicken
   stock (see page 18)

4 fl oz/125 ml/$^1$/$_2$ cup
   dry white wine

2 sachets squid or cuttlefish ink

2 tbsp chopped fresh
   flat-leaf parsley

salt and pepper

## method

**1** Heat half the oil in a large, heavy-bottom skillet over medium–high heat. When the oil is very hot, add the squid strips and stir-fry for 2–3 minutes until just cooked. Transfer to a plate and sprinkle with the lemon juice.

**2** Heat the remaining oil and butter in a large, heavy-bottom pan over medium heat. Add the garlic and chili and cook gently for 1 minute. Reduce the heat, add the rice, and mix to coat in oil and butter. Cook, stirring constantly, for 2–3 minutes, or until the grains are translucent. Pour in the wine and cook, stirring constantly, for 1 minute until reduced.

**3** Gradually add the hot stock, a ladleful at a time. Stir constantly and add more liquid as the rice absorbs each addition. Increase the heat to medium so that the liquid bubbles. Cook for 20 minutes, or until all the liquid is absorbed and the rice is creamy.

**4** Just before adding the last ladleful of stock, add the squid ink to the stock and stir to blend completely. Stir into the risotto with the reserved squid pieces and the parsley. Season to taste with salt and pepper. Serve at once.

# risotto with squid & garlic butter

## ingredients

**SERVES 4**

8–12 prepared raw baby
squid, rinsed and patted
dry on paper towels

5$^1$/$_2$ oz/150 g butter

1 tbsp olive oil

1 small onion, finely chopped

10 oz/280 g/1$^1$/$_2$ cups
Arborio rice

2 pints/1.2 liters/5 cups
simmering fish or chicken
stock (see page 18)

salt and pepper

3 garlic cloves, crushed

3 oz/85 g/$^3$/$_4$ cup freshly grated
Parmesan or
Grana Padano cheese

2 tbsp finely chopped fresh
parsley, to garnish

## method

**1** Cut the squid in half lengthwise, then score with a sharp knife, making horizontal and vertical cuts. Dice the larger tentacles.

**2** Melt 2 tablespoons of the butter with the oil in a deep pan over medium heat. Stir in the onion and cook, stirring occasionally, until soft and starting to turn golden. Do not brown. Add the rice and mix to coat in oil and butter. Cook, stirring, for 2–3 minutes, or until the grains are translucent. Add the hot stock a ladleful at a time, stirring constantly, until all the liquid is absorbed and the rice is creamy. Season to taste with salt and pepper.

**3** When the risotto is nearly cooked, melt 4 oz/ 115 g of the remaining butter in a heavy-bottom skillet. Add the garlic and cook over low heat for 2 minutes, or until soft. Increase the heat to high, add the squid, and toss for 2–3 minutes until opaque and just cooked. Remove the squid from the skillet, draining carefully and reserving the garlic butter.

**4** Remove the risotto from the heat and add the remaining butter. Mix well, then stir in the Parmesan until it melts. Spoon the risotto onto warmed serving plates and arrange the squid on top. Spoon some of the garlic butter over each portion. Sprinkle with the chopped parsley and serve at once.

# rice with seafood & squid

## ingredients

**SERVES 4**

2 tbsp vegetable or peanut oil

3 shallots, chopped finely

2 garlic cloves, chopped finely

8 oz/225 g/generous 1 cup
    jasmine rice

10 fl oz/300 ml/1¼ cups
    fish stock

4 scallions, chopped

2 tbsp Thai red curry paste

8 oz/225 g baby squid,
    cleaned and sliced thickly

8 oz/225 g white fish fillets,
    skinned and cut
    into cubes

8 oz/225 g salmon fillets,
    skinned and cut
    into cubes

4 tbsp chopped fresh cilantro

## method

**1** Heat 1 tablespoon of the oil in a wok and stir-fry the shallots and garlic for 2–3 minutes, until softened. Add the rice and stir-fry for 2–3 minutes.

**2** Add a ladleful of the stock and let simmer, adding more stock as needed, for 12–15 minutes, until tender. Transfer to a dish, let cool, and chill overnight.

**3** Heat the remaining oil in a wok and stir-fry the scallions and curry paste for 2–3 minutes. Add the squid and fish and stir-fry gently to avoid breaking up the fish. Stir in the rice and cilantro, heat through gently, and serve.

# genoese seafood risotto

## ingredients

SERVES 4

3 tbsp olive oil

9 oz/250 g mixed seafood,
  preferably raw or live,
  such as shrimp, squid,
  mussels, and clams,
  prepared as necessary

2 tbsp chopped fresh
  oregano, plus extra
  to garnish

2 oz/55 g butter

2 garlic cloves, chopped

12 oz/350 g/generous
  $1^5/_8$ cups Arborio rice

$2^1/_4$ pints/1.3 liters/generous
  $5^1/_2$ cups simmering fish
  or chicken stock
  (see page 18)

salt and pepper

2 oz/55 g/$^1/_2$ cup freshly
  grated romano or
  Parmesan cheese

## method

**1** Heat 2 tablespoons of the oil in a large skillet and add the raw or live mixed seafood. Cook over medium–high heat, stirring frequently, for 5 minutes. If the seafood is already cooked, stir-fry for 2 minutes. Remove the skillet from the heat and stir in the oregano.

**2** Heat the remaining oil with 2 tablespoons of the butter in a deep pan over medium heat until the butter has melted. Add the garlic and cook, stirring, for 1 minute. Reduce the heat, add the rice, and mix to coat in oil and butter. Cook, stirring constantly, for 2–3 minutes, or until the grains are translucent.

**3** Gradually add the hot stock, a ladleful at a time. Stir constantly and add more liquid as the rice absorbs each addition. Increase the heat to medium so that the liquid bubbles. Cook for 20 minutes, or until all the liquid is absorbed and the rice is creamy. About 5 minutes before the rice is ready, add the seafood to the pan and mix well.

**4** Remove the pan from the heat and season to taste. Add the remaining butter and mix well, then stir in the grated cheese until it melts. Spoon onto warmed plates and serve at once.

# venetian seafood risotto

## ingredients

SERVES 4

8 oz/225 g prepared raw
   shrimp, heads and
   shells reserved
2 garlic cloves, halved
1 lemon, sliced
8 oz/225 g live mussels*,
   scrubbed and debearded
8 oz/225 g live clams*,
   scrubbed
1 pint/600 ml/2$^1$/$_2$ cups water
4 oz/115 g butter
1 tbsp olive oil
1 onion, finely chopped
2 tbsp chopped fresh
   flat-leaf parsley .
12 oz/350 g/1$^3$/$_4$ cups
   Arborio rice
4 fl oz/125 ml/$^1$/$_2$ cup
   dry white wine
8 oz/225 g cleaned raw
   squid, cut into small
   pieces, or squid rings
4 tbsp Marsala
salt and pepper

* discard any mussels or
   clams that remain closed
   after cooking

## method

**1** Wrap the shrimp heads and shells in a square of cheesecloth and pound with a pestle. Put the wrapped shells and their liquid in a pan with the garlic, lemon, mussels, and clams. Add the water, cover, and bring to a boil over high heat. Cook, shaking the pan frequently, for 5 minutes until the shellfish have opened. Let cool, then shell and set aside. Strain the cooking liquid through a strainer lined with cheesecloth and add water to make 2 pints/ 1.2 liters/5 cups. Bring to a boil in a pan, then let simmer gently over low heat.

**2** Melt 2 tablespoons of butter with the olive oil in a pan. Cook the onion and half the parsley over medium heat, stirring occasionally, until softened. Reduce the heat, stir in the rice, and cook, stirring, until the grains are translucent. Add the wine and cook, stirring, for 1 minute until reduced. Add the hot cooking liquid a ladleful at a time, stirring constantly, until all the liquid is absorbed and the rice is creamy.

**3** Melt 2 oz/55 g of the remaining butter in a pan. Cook the squid, stirring frequently, for 3 minutes. Add the shrimp and cook for 2–3 minutes, until the squid is opaque and the shrimp have changed color. Add the Marsala, bring to a boil, and cook until the liquid has evaporated. Stir all the seafood into the rice, add the remaining butter and parsley, and season. Heat gently and serve at once.

# risotto with clams

## ingredients

**SERVES 6**

2 fl oz/50 ml/¼ cup olive oil

1 large onion, finely chopped

4 lb 8 oz/2 kg tiny clams,
    such as Venus, well
    scrubbed

4 fl oz/125 ml/½ cup
    dry white wine

3 garlic cloves, finely chopped

½ tsp crushed dried chili

14 oz/400 g/scant 2 cups
    Arborio rice

1 pints/1 liter/4 cups
    fish stock and 1 pint/
    600 ml/2½ cups water,
    simmering (see page 18)

3 ripe plum tomatoes, peeled
    and coarsely chopped

3 tbsp lemon juice

2 tbsp chopped fresh chervil
    or parsley

salt and pepper

## method

**1** Heat 1–2 tablespoons of the oil in a large, heavy-bottom pan over medium–high heat. Add the onion and cook, stirring constantly, for 1 minute. Add the clams and wine and cover tightly. Cook, shaking the pan frequently, for 2–3 minutes until the clams start to open. Remove from the heat and discard any clams that do not open. When cool enough to handle, remove the clams from their shells. Rinse in the cooking liquid, cover and set aside. Strain the cooking liquid through a strainer lined with paper towels and set aside.

**2** Heat the remaining oil in a large, heavy-bottom pan over medium heat. Add the garlic and chili and cook gently for 1 minute. Reduce the heat, add the rice, and mix to coat in oil. Cook, stirring constantly, for 2–3 minutes, or until the grains are translucent.

**3** Gradually add the hot stock mixture, a ladleful at a time. Stir constantly and add more liquid as the rice absorbs each addition. Increase the heat to medium so that the liquid bubbles. Cook for 20 minutes, or until all the liquid is absorbed and the rice is creamy.

**4** Stir in the tomatoes, reserved clams and their cooking liquid, the lemon juice, and chervil. Heat through gently. Season to taste with salt and pepper. Spoon the risotto onto warmed plates and serve at once.

# shrimp & asparagus risotto

## ingredients

**SERVES 4**

2 pints/1.2 liters/5 cups
vegetable stock

12 oz/375 g fresh asparagus
spears, cut into 2-inch/
5-cm lengths

2 tbsp olive oil

1 onion, finely chopped

1 garlic clove, finely chopped

12 oz/350 g/generous 1$^{1}$/$_{2}$
cups Arborio rice

1 lb/450 g raw jumbo shrimp,
shelled and deveined

2 tbsp olive paste or tapenade

2 tbsp chopped fresh basil

salt and pepper

## to garnish

fresh Parmesan cheese

fresh basil sprigs

## method

**1** Bring the stock to a boil in a large pan. Add the asparagus and cook for 3 minutes until just tender. Strain, reserving the stock, and refresh the asparagus under cold running water. Drain and set aside. Return the stock to the pan and keep simmering gently over low heat while you are cooking the risotto.

**2** Heat the olive oil in a large, heavy-bottom pan. Add the onion and cook over medium heat, stirring occasionally, for 5 minutes until softened. Add the garlic and cook for an additional 30 seconds. Reduce the heat, add the rice, and mix to coat in oil. Cook, stirring constantly, for 2–3 minutes, or until the grains are translucent.

**3** Gradually add the hot stock, a ladleful at a time. Stir constantly and add more liquid as the rice absorbs each addition. Increase the heat to medium so that the liquid bubbles. Cook for 20 minutes, until all the liquid is absorbed and the rice is creamy. Add the shrimp and asparagus when you add the last ladleful of stock.

**4** Remove the pan from the heat, stir in the olive paste and basil, and season to taste with salt and pepper. Spoon the risotto onto warmed plates and serve at once, garnished with Parmesan cheese and basil sprigs.

# fried rice with shrimp

## ingredients

SERVES 4

10$^1$/$_2$ oz/300 g/1$^1$/$_2$ cups
long-grain rice

2 eggs

4 tsp cold water

salt and pepper to taste

3 tbsp corn oil

4 scallions, sliced thinly on
the diagonal

1 garlic clove, minced

4$^1$/$_2$ oz/125 g closed-cup or
white mushrooms,
sliced thinly

2 tbsp oyster or anchovy sauce

7 oz/200 g canned water
chestnuts, drained
and sliced

9 oz/250 g cooked shelled
shrimp, thawed if frozen

finely chopped parsley,
to garnish (optional)

## method

**1** Bring a pan of lightly salted water to a boil. Sprinkle in the rice, return to a boil, then reduce the heat and let simmer for 15–20 minutes, or until tender. Drain, rinse with boiled water, then drain again. Keep warm.

**2** Beat each egg separately with 2 teaspoons of cold water and salt and pepper to taste. Heat 2 teaspoons of the corn oil in a wok or a large skillet, swirling it around until it is really hot. Pour in the first egg, swirl it around, and cook undisturbed until set. Remove to a plate or a board and repeat with the second egg. Cut the omelets into 1-inch/2.5-cm squares and set aside until required.

**3** Heat the remaining oil in the wok, and when it is really hot, add the scallions and garlic and stir-fry for 1 minute. Add the mushrooms and stir-fry for an additional 2 minutes. Stir in the oyster or anchovy sauce, and season with salt and pepper to taste. Add the water chestnuts and shrimp, and stir-fry for 2 minutes.

**4** Stir in the cooked rice and stir-fry for 1 minute, then add the omelet squares and stir-fry for 1–2 minutes more, or until piping hot. Serve immediately, garnished with chopped parsley, if you like.

# vegetable
## dishes

Vegetable-based rice dishes are excellent whether you are actually a strict vegetarian or simply do not wish to eat meat or fish every day of the week. There are many delicious and original ideas here that make marvelous talking points when you are having friends round—try the Fennel Risotto with Vodka, for example, or Beet, Dried Cherry, and Red Wine. To celebrate the arrival of the first fresh, seasonal vegetables, serve Risotto Primavera, the Italian word for spring.

If you do eat a diet based mainly on vegetables, you will know that grains and beans make a perfect nutritional combination. Try the Lima Bean and Manchego Paella, the Spicy Three-bean Paella, the Brown Rice and Vegetable Pilaf, Rice with Chana Dal, or the Kidney Bean Risotto, which is made with brown rice for maximum goodness and cashew nuts for extra protein and crunch. Remember to allow a little longer to cook brown rice—it takes about 35–40 minutes.

Vegetarians often feel left out on festive occasions where the feast is usually meat-based, but Pumpkin and Chestnut Risotto has all the elements of the winter season, and you won't hear many complaints if you serve a Crunchy Walnut Risotto, with its creamy mixture of mascarpone and dolcelatte cheeses. Pure indulgence!

# brown rice vegetable pilaf

## ingredients

**SERVES 4**

4 tbsp vegetable oil

1 red onion, finely chopped

2 tender celery stalks, leaves included, quartered lengthwise, and diced

2 carrots, coarsely grated

1 fresh green chile, seeded and finely chopped

3 scallions, green part included, finely chopped

$1^1/_2$ oz/40 g/generous $^1/_4$ cup whole almonds, sliced lengthwise

12 oz/350 g/$1^3/_4$ cups cooked brown basmati rice

$5^1/_2$ oz/150 g/$^3/_4$ cup cooked split red lentils

6 fl oz/175 ml/$^3/_4$ cup chicken or vegetable stock

5 tbsp fresh orange juice

salt and pepper

fresh celery leaves, to garnish

## method

**1** Heat 2 tablespoons of the oil in a high-sided skillet with a lid over medium heat. Add the onion. Cook for 5 minutes, or until softened.

**2** Add the celery, carrots, chile, scallions, and almonds. Stir-fry for 2 minutes, or until the vegetables are al dente but still brightly colored. Transfer to a bowl and set aside.

**3** Add the remaining oil to the skillet. Stir in the rice and lentils. Cook over medium–high heat, stirring, for 1–2 minutes, or until heated through. Reduce the heat. Stir in the stock and orange juice. Season to taste with salt and pepper.

**4** Return the vegetables to the skillet. Toss with the rice for a few minutes until heated through. Transfer to a warmed dish, garnish with celery leaves, and serve.

# red wine, herb & sun-dried tomato risotto

## ingredients

SERVES 4

1³/₄ pints/1 liter/4 cups
    vegetable stock
1³/₄ pints/1 liter/4 cups strong
    Italian red wine
1 tbsp olive oil
3 tbsp butter
1 small onion, finely chopped
450 g/1 lb/2²/₃ cups
    Arborio rice
6 sun-dried tomatoes in
    olive oil, drained and
    finely chopped
1 tbsp chopped fresh thyme,
    plus extra sprigs to garnish
1 tbsp chopped fresh parsley
salt and pepper
55 g/2 oz/¹/₂ cups freshly
    grated Parmesan or
    Grana Padano cheese,
    plus extra shavings
10–12 fresh basil leaves,
    shredded, to garnish

## method

**1** Bring the stock and wine to a boil in a pan, then reduce the heat and let simmer gently over low heat while you are cooking the risotto.

**2** Heat the oil with 2 tablespoons of the butter in a deep pan over medium heat until the butter is melted. Add the onion and cook, stirring frequently, for 5 minutes, or until softened but not browned.

**3** Add the rice, stir to coat in the butter and oil and cook, stirring constantly, for 2–3 minutes until the grains are translucent. Gradually add the hot stock, a ladleful at a time, stirring constantly. Stir in the sun-dried tomatoes, then continue to add the stock, a ladleful at a time. Cook for 20 minutes, or until all the stock has been absorbed, carefully folding in the chopped thyme and parsley 5 minutes before the end of cooking time. When the risotto is creamy but still with a little bite to the rice, season to taste.

**4** Remove the risotto from the heat and add the remaining butter. Mix well, then stir in the Parmesan cheese until it has melted. Taste and adjust the seasoning, if necessary, and serve at once, garnished with Parmesan cheese shavings, shredded basil leaves, and thyme sprigs.

# vegetable biryani

## ingredients

### SERVES 4

2 tbsp vegetable oil

3 whole cloves

3 cardamom pods, cracked

1 onion, chopped

4 oz/115 g carrots, chopped

2–3 garlic cloves, crushed

1–2 fresh red chiles, seeded
and chopped

1-inch/2.5-cm piece fresh
gingerroot, grated

4 oz/115 g cauliflower, broken
into small flowerets

6 oz/175 g broccoli, broken
into small flowerets

4 oz/115 g green beans,
chopped

14 oz/400 g canned chopped
tomatoes

5 fl oz/150 ml/$^2$/3 cup
vegetable stock

salt and pepper

4 oz/115 g okra, sliced

1 tbsp chopped fresh cilantro,
plus extra sprigs to garnish

4 oz/115 g/generous $^1$/4 cup
brown basmati rice

few saffron threads (optional)

zested lime rind, to garnish

## method

**1** Heat the oil in a large pan over low heat, add the spices, onion, carrots, garlic, chiles, and ginger and cook, stirring frequently, for 5 minutes.

**2** Add all the vegetables, except the okra, and cook, stirring frequently, for 5 minutes. Stir in the tomatoes, stock, and salt and pepper to taste and bring to a boil. Reduce the heat, cover, and let simmer for 10 minutes.

**3** Add the okra and cook for an additional 8–10 minutes, or until the vegetables are tender. Stir in the cilantro. Strain off any excess liquid and keep warm.

**4** Meanwhile, cook the rice with the saffron threads, if using, in a pan of lightly salted boiling water for about 25 minutes, or until tender. Drain and keep warm.

**5** Layer the vegetables and cooked rice in a deep dish or ovenproof bowl, packing the layers down firmly. Let stand for about 5 minutes, then invert onto a warmed serving dish and serve, garnished with zested lime rind and cilantro sprigs, with the reserved liquid.

# vegetarian paella

## ingredients

SERVES 4–6

$^1/_2$ tsp saffron threads

2 tbsp hot water

6 tbsp olive oil

1 Spanish onion, sliced

3 garlic cloves, minced

1 red bell pepper, seeded and
   sliced

1 orange bell pepper, seeded
   and sliced

1 large eggplant, cubed

7 oz/200 g/1 cup medium-
   grain paella rice

1 pint/600 ml/2$^1/_2$ cups
   vegetable stock

1 lb/450 g tomatoes, peeled
   and chopped

salt and pepper

4 oz/115 g mushrooms, sliced

4 oz/115 g green beans, halved

14 oz/400 g canned
   pinto beans

## method

**1** Put the saffron threads and water in a small bowl or cup and let infuse for a few minutes.

**2** Meanwhile, heat the oil in a paella pan or wide, shallow skillet and cook the onion over medium heat, stirring, for 2–3 minutes, or until softened. Add the garlic, bell peppers, and eggplant and cook, stirring frequently, for 5 minutes.

**3** Add the rice and cook, stirring constantly, for 1 minute, or until glossy and coated. Pour in the stock and add the tomatoes, saffron and its soaking water, and salt and pepper to taste. Bring to a boil, then reduce the heat and let simmer, shaking the skillet frequently and stirring occasionally, for 15 minutes.

**4** Stir in the mushrooms, green beans, and pinto beans with their can juices. Cook for an additional 10 minutes, then serve immediately.

# paella de verduras

## ingredients

**SERVES 4–6**

$^1/_2$ tsp saffron threads

2 tbsp hot water

3 tbsp olive oil

1 large onion, chopped

2 garlic cloves, crushed

1 tsp paprika

8 oz/225 g tomatoes, peeled
and cut into wedges

1 red bell pepper, halved and
seeded, then broiled,
peeled, and sliced

1 green bell pepper, halved
and seeded, then broiled,
peeled, and sliced

15 oz/425 g canned
chickpeas, drained

12 oz/350 g/generous
1$^1/_2$ cups medium-grain
paella rice

2$^1/_4$ pints/1.3 liters/5$^1/_2$ cups
simmering vegetable stock

2 oz/55 g/$^3/_8$ cup shelled peas

5$^1/_2$ oz/150 g fresh asparagus
spears, blanched

1 tbsp chopped fresh flat-leaf
parsley, plus extra
to garnish

salt and pepper

## method

**1** Put the saffron threads and water in a small bowl and let infuse for a few minutes.

**2** Meanwhile, heat the oil in a paella pan and cook the onion over medium heat, stirring, for 2–3 minutes, or until softened. Add the garlic, paprika, and saffron and its soaking liquid and cook, stirring, for 1 minute. Add the tomatoes, bell peppers, and chickpeas and cook, stirring, for an additional 2 minutes.

**3** Add the rice and cook, stirring constantly, for 1 minute, or until glossy and coated. Pour in most of the hot stock and bring to a boil. Reduce the heat and let simmer, uncovered, for 10 minutes. Do not stir during cooking, but shake the pan once or twice. Add the peas, asparagus, and parsley and season to taste with salt and pepper. Shake the pan and cook for an additional 10–15 minutes, or until the rice grains are plump and cooked. Pour in a little more hot stock if necessary, then shake the pan to spread the liquid through the paella.

**4** When all the liquid has been absorbed and you detect a faint toasty aroma coming from the rice, remove from the heat immediately to prevent burning. Cover the pan with a clean dish towel or foil and let stand for 5 minutes. Sprinkle over chopped parsley to garnish and serve direct from the pan.

# spicy three-bean paella

## ingredients

SERVES 4-6

$^{1}/_{2}$ tsp saffron threads

2 tbsp hot water

3 tbsp olive oil

1 large red onion, minced

2 garlic cloves, crushed

1 small fresh red chile,
    seeded and minced

1 tsp paprika

$^{1}/_{4}$ tsp cayenne pepper

1 red bell pepper, halved and
    seeded, then broiled,
    peeled, and sliced

8 oz/225 g tomatoes, peeled
    and cut into wedges

6 oz/175 g canned chickpeas
    (drained weight)

6 oz/175 g canned red kidney
    beans (drained weight)

6 oz/175 g canned lima
    beans (drained weight)

12 oz/350 g/generous
    1$^{1}/_{2}$ cups medium-grain
    paella rice

2$^{1}/_{4}$ pints/1.3 liters/5$^{1}/_{2}$ cups
    hot vegetable stock

5$^{1}/_{2}$ oz/150 g green beans,
    blanched

1 tbsp chopped fresh flat-leaf
    parsley, plus extra
    to garnish

salt and pepper

lemon wedges, to serve

## method

**1** Put the saffron threads and water in a small bowl and let infuse for a few minutes.

**2** Meanwhile, heat the oil in a paella pan and cook the onion over medium heat, stirring, for 2–3 minutes, or until softened. Add the garlic, chile, paprika, cayenne pepper, and saffron and its soaking liquid and cook, stirring constantly, for 1 minute. Add the red bell peppers, tomatoes, chickpeas, kidney beans, and lima beans and cook, stirring, for an additional 2 minutes.

**3** Add the rice and cook, stirring constantly, for 1 minute, or until glossy and coated. Pour in most of the hot stock and bring to a boil, then let simmer, uncovered, for 10 minutes. Do not stir during cooking, but shake the pan once or twice. Add the green beans and the parsley and season to taste. Shake the pan and cook for 10–15 minutes, or until the rice grains are plump and cooked. If the liquid is absorbed too quickly, pour in a little more hot stock, then shake the pan to spread the liquid through the paella. Do not stir it in.

**4** When all the liquid has been absorbed and you detect a faint toasty aroma coming from the rice, remove from the heat. Cover the pan with foil and let stand for 5 minutes. Sprinkle over chopped parsley to garnish and serve with the lemon wedges.

# artichoke paella

## ingredients

**SERVES 4–6**

$^1/_2$ tsp saffron threads

2 tbsp hot water

3 tbsp olive oil

1 large onion, chopped

1 zucchini, coarsely chopped

2 garlic cloves, crushed

$^1/_4$ tsp cayenne pepper

8 oz/225 g tomatoes, peeled
  and cut into wedges

15 oz/425 g canned
  chickpeas, drained

15 oz/425 g canned
  artichokes hearts, drained
  and coarsely sliced

12 oz/350 g/generous
  1$^1/_2$ cups medium-grain
  paella rice

2$^1/_4$ pints/1.3 liters/5$^1/_2$ cups
  simmering vegetable stock

5$^1/_2$ oz/150 g green beans,
  blanched

salt and pepper

1 lemon, cut into wedges,
  to serve

## method

**1** Put the saffron threads and water in a small bowl and let infuse for a few minutes.

**2** Meanwhile, heat the oil in a paella pan and cook the onion and zucchini over medium heat, stirring, for 2–3 minutes, or until softened. Add the garlic, cayenne pepper, and saffron and its soaking liquid and cook, stirring constantly, for 1 minute. Add the tomato wedges, chickpeas, and artichokes and cook, stirring, for an additional 2 minutes.

**3** Add the rice and cook, stirring constantly, for 1 minute, or until the rice is glossy and coated. Pour in most of the hot stock and bring to a boil, then let simmer, uncovered, for 10 minutes. Do not stir during cooking, but shake the pan once or twice. Add the green beans and season to taste. Shake the pan and cook for an additional 10–15 minutes, or until the rice grains are plump and cooked. If the liquid is absorbed too quickly, pour in a little more hot stock, then shake the pan to spread the liquid through the paella. Do not stir it in.

**4** When all the liquid has been absorbed and you detect a faint toasty aroma coming from the rice, remove from the heat immediately to prevent burning. Cover the pan with a clean dish towel or foil and let stand for 5 minutes. Serve direct from the pan with the lemon wedges to squeeze over the rice.

# lima bean & manchego paella

## ingredients

**SERVES 4–6**

$^1/_2$ tsp saffron threads

2 tbsp hot water

3 tbsp olive oil

2 red onions, chopped

2 garlic cloves, crushed

1 tsp paprika

8 oz/225 g tomatoes, peeled
    and cut into wedges

1 red bell pepper, halved and
    seeded, then broiled,
    peeled, and sliced

15 oz/425 g canned lima
    beans, drained

12 oz/350 g/generous
    1$^1/_2$ cups medium-grain
    paella rice

2$^1/_4$ pints/1.3 liters/5$^1/_2$ cups
    simmering vegetable stock

2 oz/55 g/$^3/_8$ cup shelled peas

2 oz/55 g/$^3/_8$ cup corn kernels

20 black olives, pitted and
    halved (optional)

1 tbsp chopped fresh flat-leaf
    parsley

1 tbsp chopped fresh thyme

salt and pepper

3$^1/_2$ oz/100 g Spanish
    manchego cheese

1 lemon, cut into wedges,
    to serve

## method

**1** Put the saffron threads and water in a small bowl and let infuse for a few minutes.

**2** Meanwhile, heat the oil in a paella pan and cook the onions over medium heat, stirring, for 2–3 minutes, or until softened. Add the garlic, paprika, and saffron and its soaking liquid and cook, stirring constantly, for 1 minute. Add the tomatoes, bell peppers, and lima beans and cook, stirring, for an additional 2 minutes.

**3** Add the rice and cook, stirring constantly, for 1 minute, or until glossy and coated. Pour in most of the hot stock and bring to a boil. Reduce the heat and let simmer, uncovered, for 10 minutes. Do not stir during cooking, but shake the pan once or twice. Add the peas, corn, olives, if using, and herbs and season to taste with salt and pepper. Shake the pan and cook for an additional 10–15 minutes, or until the rice grains are plump and cooked. If the liquid is absorbed too quickly, pour in a little more hot stock, then shake the pan to spread the liquid through the paella. Do not stir it in.

**4** When all the liquid has been absorbed and you detect a faint toasty aroma coming from the rice, remove from the heat. Cover the pan with foil and let stand for 5 minutes.

**5** Meanwhile, use a potato peeler to shave the cheese. Sprinkle the cheese shavings over the paella and serve with the lemon wedges.

# rice with chana dal

## ingredients

SERVES 6

4 tbsp ghee

2 onions, sliced

1 tsp finely chopped fresh
gingerroot

1 tsp crushed fresh garlic

$1/2$ tsp ground turmeric

2 tsp salt

$1/2$ tsp chili powder

1 tsp garam masala

5 tbsp plain yogurt

8 oz/225 g/$7/8$ cup chana dal,
rinsed and soaked for
3 hours

$2^{1}/4$ pints/1.3 liters/
$5^{1}/2$ cups water

5 fl oz/150 ml/$2/3$ cup milk

1 tsp saffron threads

3 black cardamoms

3 black cumin seeds

1 lb/450 g/2 cups
basmati rice, rinsed and
any stones removed

3 tbsp lemon juice

2 fresh green chiles, sliced

2–3 tbsp fresh cilantro leaves

chopped fresh cilantro,
to garnish

## method

**1** Heat the ghee in a heavy-bottom skillet. Add the onions and cook until golden brown. Using a slotted spoon, transfer half of the onion with a little of the ghee to a bowl and set aside.

**2** Add the ginger, garlic, turmeric, half the salt, the chili powder, and the garam masala to the skillet and stir-fry for 5 minutes. Stir in the yogurt and add the chana dal and 5 fl oz/ 150 ml/$2/3$ cup of the water. Cover and cook for 15 minutes. Remove the skillet from the heat and set aside. Boil the milk with the saffron threads and set aside.

**3** Meanwhile, in a separate pan, boil the remaining water and add the remaining salt and the cardamoms, cumin seeds, and rice. Cook, stirring, until the rice is half-cooked, then drain. Transfer half of the rice to a bowl and set aside, and return the rest to the pan. Pour the dal mixture over the rice in the pan. Sprinkle over half of the reserved cooked onion and half of the saffron milk, lemon juice, chiles, and cilantro leaves. Place the reserved rice on top of this and the rest of the cooked onion, saffron milk, lemon juice, chiles, and cilantro leaves on top. Cover tightly with a lid and cook for 20 minutes over very low heat. Mix well, garnish with chopped cilantro and serve.

# lentil & rice casserole

## ingredients

**SERVES 4**

8 oz/225g/generous 1 cup
  red split lentils, rinsed
2 oz/55 g/$^1/_4$ cup long-grain
  rice
2 pints/1.2 liters/5 cups
  vegetable stock
1 leek, cut into chunks
3 garlic cloves, crushed
14 oz/400 g canned chopped
  tomatoes
1 tsp each of ground cumin,
  chili powder,
  and garam masala
1 red bell pepper, seeded and
  sliced
3$^1/_2$ oz/100 g small broccoli
  florets
8 baby corn cobs, halved
  lengthwise
2 oz/55 g green beans, halved
1 tbsp shredded fresh basil
salt and pepper
fresh basil sprigs, to garnish

## method

**1** Place the lentils, rice, and vegetable stock in a flameproof casserole and cook over low heat, stirring occasionally, for 20 minutes.

**2** Add the leek and garlic to the pan with the tomatoes and their juices, ground spices, bell pepper, broccoli, baby corn, and green beans and stir well to mix.

**3** Bring the mixture to a boil, then reduce the heat, cover, and simmer for an additional 10–15 minutes, until the vegetables are tender. Add the shredded basil and season to taste with salt and pepper. Garnish with basil sprigs and serve.

# stuffed bell peppers

## ingredients

**MAKES 6**

6 tbsp olive oil, plus a little
extra for rubbing on peppers

2 onions, chopped finely

2 garlic cloves, crushed

5 oz/140 g/²/₃ cup Spanish
short-grain rice

2 oz/55 g/²/₃ cup raisins

2 oz/55 g/¹/₂ cup pine nuts

3 tbsp fresh parsley,
chopped finely

salt and pepper

1 tbsp tomato paste dissolved
in 1¹/₄ pints/700 ml/
3 cups hot water

4–6 red, green, or yellow bell
peppers (or a mix of
colors), or 6 of the long,
Mediterranean variety

## method

**1** Heat the oil in a shallow, heavy-bottom flameproof casserole. Add the onions and cook for about 3 minutes. Add the garlic and cook for an additional 2 minutes, or until the onions are soft but not brown.

**2** Stir in the rice, raisins, and pine nuts until all are coated in the oil, then add half the parsley and season to taste. Stir in the dissolved tomato paste and bring to a boil. Reduce the heat and let simmer, uncovered, for 20 minutes, shaking the casserole frequently, or until the rice is tender, the liquid is absorbed, and small holes appear on the surface: watch carefully because the raisins can catch and burn easily. Stir in the remaining parsley, then set aside and let cool slightly.

**3** While the rice is simmering, cut the top off each bell pepper and set aside. Remove the core and seeds from each pepper. Divide the stuffing equally between the bell peppers. Use wooden toothpicks to secure the tops back in place. Lightly rub each bell pepper with oil and arrange in a single layer in a baking dish. Bake in a preheated oven, 400°F/ 200°C, for 30 minutes, or until the bell peppers are tender. Serve hot or let cool to room temperature.

# spiced risotto cakes with mango, lime & cream cheese

## ingredients

**MAKES 3**

3 oz/85 g onion, finely chopped

3 oz/85 g leek, finely chopped

1 oz/25g/$^1$/$_8$ cup Arborio rice

18 fl oz/500 ml/scant 2$^1$/$_2$ cups vegetable stock

3 oz/85 g/scant $^1$/$_2$ cup grated zucchini

1 tbsp fresh basil, chopped

1 oz/25g/$^1$/$_2$ cup fresh whole wheat breadcrumbs

vegetable oil spray

salad greens, to serve

### filling

1$^3$/$_4$ oz/50 g/scant $^1$/$_4$ cup cream cheese

1$^3$/$_4$ oz/50 g mango, diced

1 tsp finely grated lime zest

1 tsp lime juice

pinch of cayenne pepper

## method

**1** Heat a large, nonstick pan over high heat, add the onion and leek, and cook, stirring constantly, for 2–3 minutes, or until softened but not colored.

**2** Add the rice and stock, bring to a boil, then continue to boil, stirring constantly, for 2 minutes. Reduce the heat and cook for an additional 15 minutes, stirring every 2–3 minutes. When the rice is nearly cooked and has absorbed all the stock, stir in the zucchini and basil and cook, continuing to stir, over high heat for an additional 5–10 minutes or until the mixture is sticky and dry. Turn out onto a plate and let cool.

**3** Meanwhile, to make the filling, mix the cream cheese, mango, lime zest and juice, and cayenne together in a bowl.

**4** Divide the cooled rice mixture into 3 and form into cakes. Make an indentation in the center of each cake and fill with 1 tbsp of the filling. Mold the sides up and over to seal in the filling, then reshape with a palette knife. Coat each cake with bread crumbs and arrange on a nonstick baking sheet. Spray each cake lightly with oil and bake in a preheated oven, 400°F/200°C, for 15–20 minutes, or until a light golden brown color. Serve with salad greens.

# roasted butternut squash risotto

## ingredients

**SERVES 4**

1 lb 5 oz/600 g butternut
   squash or pumpkin,
   peeled and cut into
   bite-size pieces

4 tbsp olive oil

1 tsp honey

2 tbsp fresh basil

2 tbsp fresh oregano

1 tbsp butter

2 onions, finely chopped

1 lb/450 g/2 cups Arborio rice

6 fl oz/175 ml/³/₄ cup
   dry white wine

2 pints/1.2 liters/5 cups
   vegetable stock

salt and pepper

## method

**1** Put the squash into a roasting pan. Mix 1 tablespoon of the oil with the honey and spoon over the squash. Turn the squash to coat it in the mixture. Roast in a preheated oven, 400°F/200°C, for 30–35 minutes, or until tender.

**2** Meanwhile, put the basil and oregano into a food processor with 2 tablespoons of the remaining oil and process until finely chopped and blended. Set aside.

**3** Heat the butter and remaining oil in a large, heavy-bottom pan over medium heat. Add the onions and cook, stirring occasionally, for 8 minutes, or until soft and golden. Add the rice and cook for 2 minutes, stirring to coat the grains in the oil mixture.

**4** Pour in the wine and bring to a boil. Reduce the heat slightly and cook until the wine is almost absorbed. Add the stock, a little at a time, and cook over medium–low heat, stirring constantly, for 20 minutes.

**5** Gently stir in the herb oil and squash until thoroughly mixed into the rice and cook for an additional 5 minutes, or until the rice is creamy and cooked but retaining a little bite in the center of the grain. Season well with salt and pepper before serving.

# parmesan cheese risotto with mushrooms

## ingredients

SERVES 4

2 tbsp olive oil or vegetable oil

8 oz/225 g/1 cup Arborio rice

1³/4 pints/1 liter/4 cups
   simmering vegetable or
   chicken stock
   (see page 18)

salt and pepper

2 garlic cloves, crushed

1 onion, chopped

2 celery stalks, chopped

1 red or green bell pepper,
   seeded and chopped

8 oz/225 g mushrooms,
   thinly sliced

1 tbsp chopped fresh oregano
   or 1 tsp dried oregano

2 oz/55g/¹/4 cup sun-dried
   tomatoes in olive oil,
   drained and chopped
   (optional)

2 oz/55 g/¹/2 cup finely grated
   Parmesan cheese

fresh flat-leaf parsley sprigs or
   bay leaves, to garnish

## method

**1** Heat the oil in a deep pan. Add the rice and cook over low heat, stirring constantly, for 2–3 minutes, until the grains are thoroughly coated in oil and translucent.

**2** Add the garlic, onion, celery, and bell pepper and cook, stirring frequently, for 5 minutes. Add the mushrooms and cook for 3–4 minutes. Stir in the oregano.

**3** Gradually add the hot stock, a ladleful at a time. Stir constantly and add more liquid as the rice absorbs each addition. Increase the heat to medium so that the liquid bubbles. Cook for 20 minutes, or until all the liquid is absorbed and the rice is creamy. Add the sun-dried tomatoes, if using, 5 minutes before the end of the cooking time and season to taste.

**4** Remove the risotto from the heat and stir in half the Parmesan until it melts. Transfer the risotto to warmed plates. Top with the remaining cheese, garnish with flat-leaf parsley or bay leaves, and serve at once.

# crunchy walnut risotto

## ingredients

SERVES 4

1 tbsp olive oil

2$^1$/$_2$ oz/70 g butter

1 small onion,
　　finely chopped

10 oz/280 g/1$^1$/$_2$ cups
　　Arborio rice

2 pints/1.2 liters/5 cups
　　simmering vegetable or
　　chicken stock
　　(see page 18)

salt and pepper

4 oz/115 g/1 cup
　　walnut halves

3 oz/85 g/$^3$/$_4$ cup freshly
　　grated Parmesan or Grana
　　Padano cheese

2oz/55 g/$^1$/$_4$ cup mascarpone
　　cheese

2 oz/55 g Gorgonzola cheese,
　　diced

## method

**1** Heat the oil with 2 tablespoons of the butter in a deep pan over medium heat until the butter has melted. Add the onion and cook, stirring occasionally, for 5–7 minutes, or until soft and starting to turn golden. Do not brown.

**2** Reduce the heat, add the rice, and mix to coat in oil and butter. Cook, stirring constantly, for 2–3 minutes, or until the grains are translucent.

**3** Gradually add the hot stock, a ladleful at a time. Stir constantly and add more liquid as the rice absorbs each addition. Increase the heat to medium so that the liquid bubbles. Cook for 20 minutes, or until all the liquid is absorbed and the rice is creamy. Season to taste with salt and pepper.

**4** Melt 2 tablespoons of the remaining butter in a skillet over medium heat. Add the walnuts and toss for 2–3 minutes, or until just starting to brown.

**5** Remove the risotto from the heat and add the remaining butter. Mix well, then stir in the Parmesan, mascarpone, and Gorgonzola until they melt, along with most of the walnuts. Spoon the risotto onto warmed plates, sprinkle with the remaining walnuts, and serve.

# risotto with four cheeses

## ingredients

**SERVES 6**

1¹/₂ oz/40 g unsalted butter

1 onion, chopped finely

12 oz/350 g/generous
    1¹/₂ cups Arborio rice

7 fl oz/200 ml/scant 1 cup
    dry white wine

1³/₄ pints/1 liter/4 cups
    simmering vegetable stock
    (see page 18)

2 oz/55 g/¹/₂ cup Gorgonzola
    cheese, crumbled

2 oz/55 g/¹/₂ cup freshly
    grated Taleggio cheese

2 oz/55 g/¹/₂ cup freshly
    grated fontina cheese

2 oz/55 g/¹/₂ cup freshly
    grated Parmesan cheese

salt and pepper

2 tbsp chopped fresh flat-leaf
    parsley, to garnish

## method

**1** Melt the butter in a large, heavy-bottom pan. Add the onion and cook over low heat, stirring occasionally, for 5 minutes, until softened. Add the rice and cook, stirring constantly, for 2–3 minutes, until all the grains are thoroughly coated and glistening.

**2** Add the wine and cook, stirring constantly, until it has almost completely evaporated. Add a ladleful of the hot stock and cook, stirring constantly, until all the stock has been absorbed. Continue cooking, stirring and adding the stock, a ladleful at a time, for about 20 minutes, or until the rice is tender and the liquid has been absorbed.

**3** Remove the pan from the heat and stir in the Gorgonzola, Taleggio, fontina, and about one-quarter of the Parmesan until melted. Season to taste with salt and pepper. Transfer the risotto to a warmed serving dish, sprinkle with the remaining Parmesan, garnish with the parsley, and serve immediately.

# pumpkin & chesnut risotto

## ingredients

**SERVES 4**

1 tbsp olive oil

3 tbsp butter

1 small onion,
    finely chopped

8 oz/225 g pumpkin, diced

8 oz/225 g chestnuts, cooked
    and shelled

12 oz/350 g/1$^1$/$_2$ cups
    Arborio rice

5 fl oz/150 ml/$^2$/$_3$ cup
    dry white wine

1 tsp crumbled saffron
    threads (optional)

1$^3$/$_4$ pints/1 liter/4 cups
    simmering vegetable or
    chicken stock
    (see page 18)

salt and pepper

3 oz/85 g/$^3$/$_4$ cup freshly grated
    Parmesan or
    Grana Padano cheese

## method

**1** Heat the oil with 2 tablespoons of the butter in a deep pan over medium heat until the butter has melted. Stir in the onion and pumpkin and cook, stirring occasionally, for 5 minutes, or until the onion is soft and starting to turn golden and the pumpkin begins to color. Coarsely chop the chestnuts and add to the mixture. Stir thoroughly to coat.

**2** Reduce the heat, add the rice, and mix to coat in oil and butter. Cook, stirring constantly, for 2–3 minutes, or until the grains are translucent. Add the wine and cook, stirring constantly, for 1 minute until it has reduced.

**3** If using the saffron threads, dissolve them in 4 tablespoons of the hot stock and add the liquid to the rice after the wine has been absorbed. Cook, stirring constantly, until the liquid has been absorbed.

**4** Gradually add the hot stock, a ladleful at a time. Stir constantly and add more liquid as the rice absorbs each addition. Increase the heat to medium so that the liquid bubbles. Cook for 20 minutes, or until all the liquid is absorbed and the rice is creamy. Season to taste.

**5** Remove the risotto from the heat and add the remaining butter. Mix well, then stir in the Parmesan until it melts. Adjust the seasoning if necessary, spoon the risotto onto 4 warmed plates, and serve at once.

# risotto primavera

## ingredients

**SERVES 6–8**

8 oz/225 g fresh thin
    asparagus spears
4 tbsp olive oil
6 oz/175 g young green
    beans, cut into 1-inch/
    2.5-cm lengths
6 oz/175 g young zucchini,
    quartered and cut into
    1-inch/2.5-cm lengths
8 oz/225 g/generous
    1$^{1}$/$_{2}$ cups shelled
    fresh peas
1 onion, finely chopped
1–2 garlic cloves, finely
    chopped
12 oz/350 g/1$^{3}$/$_{4}$ cups
    Arborio rice
2$^{3}$/$_{4}$ pints/1.5 liters/generous
    6$^{1}$/$_{3}$ cups simmering
    chicken or vegetable stock
    (see page 18)
4 scallions, cut into
    1-inch/2.5-cm lengths
salt and pepper
2 oz/55 g butter
4 oz/115 g/1 cup freshly
    grated Parmesan cheese
2 tbsp snipped fresh chives
2 tbsp shredded fresh basil
scallions, to garnish (optional)

## method

**1** Trim the woody ends of the asparagus and cut off the tips. Cut the stems into 1-inch/2.5-cm pieces and set aside with the tips.

**2** Heat 2 tablespoons of the oil in a large skillet over high heat until very hot. Add the asparagus, beans, zucchini, and peas and stir-fry for 3–4 minutes until they are bright green and just starting to soften. Set aside.

**3** Heat the remaining oil in a large, heavy-bottom pan over medium heat. Add the onion and cook, stirring occasionally, for 3 minutes, or until it starts to soften. Stir in the garlic and cook, while stirring, for 30 seconds. Reduce the heat, add the rice, and mix to coat in oil. Cook, stirring constantly, for 2–3 minutes, or until the grains are translucent.

**4** Gradually add the hot stock, a ladleful at a time. Stir constantly and add more liquid as the rice absorbs each addition. Increase the heat to medium so that the liquid bubbles. Cook for 20 minutes, or until all but 2 tablespoons of the liquid is absorbed and the rice is creamy.

**5** Stir in the stir-fried vegetables, onion mixture, and scallions with the remaining stock. Cook for 2 minutes, stirring frequently, then season to taste. Stir in the butter, Parmesan, chives, and basil. Remove the pan from the heat and serve the risotto at once, garnished with scallions, if liked.

# asparagus & sun-dried tomato risotto

## ingredients

**SERVES 4**

3 tbsp butter

1 tbsp olive oil

1 small onion, finely chopped

6 sun-dried tomatoes, thinly sliced

10 oz/280 g/1$^1$/$_2$ cups Arborio rice

5 fl oz/150 ml/$^2$/$_3$ cup dry white wine

1$^3$/$_4$ pints/1 liter/4 cups simmering vegetable stock (see page 18)

salt and pepper

8 oz/225 g fresh asparagus spears, cooked

3 oz/85 g/$^3$/$_4$ cup freshly grated Parmesan or Grana Padano cheese

thinly pared lemon rind, to garnish

## method

**1** Melt 2 tablespoons of the butter with the oil in a deep pan over medium heat. Stir in the onion and sun-dried tomatoes, and cook, stirring occasionally, for 5 minutes until the onion is soft and starting to turn golden. Do not brown. Reduce the heat, add the rice, and mix to coat in oil and butter. Cook, stirring constantly, for 2–3 minutes, or until the grains are translucent. Add the wine and cook, stirring constantly, until it has reduced.

**2** Gradually add the hot stock, a ladleful at a time. Stir constantly and add more liquid as the rice absorbs each addition. Increase the heat to medium so that the liquid bubbles. Cook for 20 minutes, or until all the liquid is absorbed and the rice is creamy. Season to taste.

**3** Meanwhile, cut most of the asparagus into pieces about 1 inch/2.5 cm long. Keep several spears whole for garnishing. Carefully fold the cut pieces of asparagus into the risotto for the last 5 minutes of cooking time.

**4** Remove the risotto from the heat and add the remaining butter. Mix well, then stir in the Parmesan until it melts. Spoon the risotto onto individual warmed serving dishes and garnish with whole spears of asparagus. Sprinkle the lemon rind on top and serve.

# fennel risotto with vodka

## ingredients

**SERVES 4–6**

2 large fennel bulbs

2 tbsp vegetable oil

3 oz/85 g butter

1 large onion,
    finely chopped

12 oz/350 g/1³/₄ cups
    Arborio rice

5 fl oz/150 ml/²/₃ cup vodka

2¹/₄ pints/1.3 liters/generous
    5¹/₂ cups simmering
    chicken or vegetable stock
    (see page 18)

salt and pepper

5–6 tbsp lemon juice

2¹/₄ oz/60 g/generous ¹/₂ cup
    freshly grated
    Parmesan cheese

## method

**1** Trim the fennel, reserving the fronds for the garnish, if desired. Cut the bulbs in half lengthwise and remove the V-shaped cores. Coarsely chop the flesh. (If you like, add any of the fennel trimmings to the stock for extra flavor.)

**2** Heat the oil with half the butter in a large heavy-bottom pan over medium heat until the butter has melted. Add the onion and fennel and cook, stirring occasionally, for 5 minutes, or until the vegetables are softened. Reduce the heat, add the rice, and mix to coat in oil and butter. Cook, stirring constantly, for 2–3 minutes, or until the grains are translucent. Pour in the vodka and cook, stirring constantly, for 1 minute until reduced.

**3** Gradually add the hot stock, a ladleful at a time. Stir constantly and add more liquid as the rice absorbs each addition. Increase the heat to medium so that the liquid bubbles. Cook for 20 minutes, or until all the liquid is absorbed and the rice is creamy. Season to taste.

**4** Remove the risotto from the heat and add the remaining butter and lemon juice to taste. Mix well, then stir in the Parmesan until it melts. Serve at once, garnished with the reserved fennel fronds, if using.

# risotto with artichoke hearts

## ingredients

**SERVES 4**

8 oz/225 g canned artichoke
hearts
1 tbsp olive oil
3 tbsp butter
1 small onion, finely chopped
10 oz/280 g/1$^1$/$_2$ cups
Arborio rice
2 pints/1.2 liters/5 cups
simmering chicken or
vegetable stock
(see page 18)
salt and pepper
3 oz/85 g/$^3$/$_4$ cup freshly grated
Parmesan or
Grana Padano cheese
fresh flat-leaf parsley sprigs,
to garnish

## method

**1** Drain the artichoke hearts, reserving the liquid, and cut them into fourths.

**2** Heat the oil with 2 tablespoons of the butter in a deep pan over medium heat until the butter has melted. Stir in the onion and cook gently, stirring occasionally, for 5 minutes, or until soft and starting to turn golden. Do not brown. Add the rice and mix to coat in oil and butter. Cook, stirring constantly, for 2–3 minutes, or until the grains are translucent.

**3** Gradually add the artichoke liquid and the hot stock, a ladle at a time. Stir constantly and add more liquid as the rice absorbs each addition. Increase the heat to medium so that the liquid bubbles. Cook for 15 minutes, then add the artichoke hearts. Cook for an additional 5 minutes, or until all the liquid is absorbed and the rice is creamy. Season to taste with salt and pepper.

**4** Remove the risotto from the heat and add the remaining butter. Mix well, then stir in the Parmesan until it melts. Taste and adjust the seasoning, if necessary. Spoon the risotto into warmed bowls, garnish with parsley sprigs, and serve at once.

# blue cheese risotto

## ingredients

**SERVES 4**

3 tbsp butter

1 tbsp olive oil

1 small onion,
  finely chopped

2 oz/55 g rindless bacon or
  vegetarian bacon
  slices, diced

10 oz/280 g/1$^{1}$/$_{2}$ cups
  Arborio rice

2 pints/1.2 liters/5 cups
  simmering vegetable or
  chicken stock
  (see page 18)

salt and pepper

4 oz/115 g Gorgonzola or
  dolcelatte cheese

## method

**1** Melt 2 tablespoons of the butter with the oil in a deep pan over low heat. Stir in the onion and bacon and cook, stirring occasionally, for 5 minutes, or until the bacon is just starting to brown and the onion is soft. Add the rice and mix to coat in oil and butter. Cook, stirring constantly, for 2–3 minutes, or until the grains are translucent.

**2** Gradually add the hot stock, a ladleful at a time. Stir constantly and add more liquid as the rice absorbs each addition. Increase the heat to medium so that the liquid bubbles. Cook for 20 minutes, or until all the liquid is absorbed and the rice is creamy. Season to taste.

**3** Remove the risotto from the heat and add the remaining butter. Mix well, then crumble in half the blue cheese and stir well until it melts. Season well with plenty of pepper.

**4** Spoon the risotto onto 4 warmed individual plates. Crumble or dice the remaining blue cheese and sprinkle it over the top of the risotto before serving.

# kidney bean risotto

## ingredients

SERVES 4

4 tbsp olive oil

1 onion, chopped

2 garlic cloves, finely chopped

6 oz/175 g/generous $^3/_4$ cup
   brown rice

1 pint/600 ml/2$^1/_2$ cups
   vegetable stock

1 red bell pepper, seeded
   and chopped

2 celery stalks, sliced

8 oz/225 g cremini
   mushrooms, thinly sliced

15 oz/425 g canned red
   kidney beans, drained
   and rinsed

3 tbsp chopped fresh parsley,
   plus extra to garnish

2 oz/55 g/scant $^3/_8$ cup
   cashews

salt and pepper

## method

**1** Heat half the oil in a large, heavy-bottom pan. Add the onion and cook, stirring occasionally, for 5 minutes, or until softened. Add half the garlic and cook, stirring frequently, for 2 minutes, then add the rice and stir for 1 minute, or until the grains are thoroughly coated with the oil.

**2** Add the stock and a pinch of salt and bring to a boil, stirring constantly. Reduce the heat, cover, and let simmer for 35–40 minutes, or until all the liquid has been absorbed.

**3** Meanwhile, heat the remaining oil in a heavy-bottom skillet. Add the bell pepper and celery and cook, stirring frequently, for 5 minutes. Add the sliced mushrooms and the remaining garlic and cook, stirring frequently, for 4–5 minutes.

**4** Stir the rice into the skillet. Add the beans, parsley, and cashews. Season to taste with salt and pepper and cook, stirring constantly, until hot. Transfer to a warmed serving dish, sprinkle with extra parsley, and serve at once.

# risotto with roasted vegetables

## ingredients

SERVES 4

1 tbsp olive oil

3 tbsp butter

1 small onion, finely chopped

10 oz/280 g/1$^1$/$_2$ cups
   Arborio rice

2 pints/1.2 liters/5 cups
   simmering chicken or
   vegetable stock
   (see page 18)

8 oz/225 g roasted
   vegetables, such as bell
   peppers, zucchini, and
   eggplant, cut into chunks

salt and pepper

3 oz/85 g/$^3$/$_4$ cup freshly
   grated Parmesan or
   Grana Padano cheese

2 tbsp finely chopped fresh
   herbs, to garnish

## method

**1** Heat the oil with 2 tablespoons of the butter in a deep pan over medium heat until the butter has melted. Add the onion and cook, stirring occasionally, for 5 minutes, until soft and starting to turn golden. Do not brown. Reduce the heat, add the rice, and mix to coat in oil and butter. Cook, stirring constantly, for 2–3 minutes, or until the grains are translucent.

**2** Gradually add the hot stock, a ladleful at a time. Stir constantly and add more liquid as the rice absorbs each addition. Increase the heat to medium so that the liquid bubbles. Cook for 15 minutes, then add most of the roasted vegetables, setting aside a few pieces to use as a garnish. Cook for an additional 5 minutes, or until all the liquid is absorbed and the rice is creamy. Season to taste with salt and pepper.

**3** Remove the risotto from the heat and add the remaining butter. Mix well, then stir in the Parmesan until it melts. Spoon the risotto onto warmed individual plates, arrange vegetables around it or on top to garnish, and then sprinkle with fresh herbs before serving at once.

# wild mushroom risotto

## ingredients

**SERVES 6**

2 oz/55 g/$^1$/$_2$ cup dried porcini
   or morel mushrooms
about 1 lb 2 oz/500 g mixed
   fresh wild mushrooms,
   such as porcini, horse
   mushrooms, and
   chanterelles, halved
   if large
4 tbsp olive oil
3–4 garlic cloves,
   finely chopped
2 oz/55 g butter
1 onion, finely chopped
12 oz/350 g/1$^3$/$_4$ cups Arborio
   rice
2 fl oz/50 ml/$^1$/$_4$ cup dry
   white vermouth
2 pints/1.2 liters/5 cups
   simmering chicken or
   vegetable stock
salt and pepper
4 oz/115 g/1 cup freshly
   grated Parmesan cheese
4 tbsp chopped fresh
   flat-leaf parsley

## method

**1** Place the dried mushrooms in a heatproof bowl and add boiling water to cover. Set aside to soak for 30 minutes, then carefully lift out and pat dry. Strain the soaking liquid through a strainer lined with paper towels and set aside.

**2** Trim the fresh mushrooms and gently brush clean. Heat 3 tablespoons of the oil in a large skillet. Add the fresh mushrooms and stir-fry for 1–2 minutes. Add the garlic and the soaked mushrooms and cook, stirring frequently, for 2 minutes. Transfer to a plate.

**3** Heat the remaining oil and half the butter in a pan. Add the onion and cook over medium heat, stirring, until softened. Reduce the heat, add the rice, and mix to coat in oil and butter. Cook, stirring, for 2–3 minutes, or until the grains are translucent. Add the vermouth and cook, stirring, for 1 minute until reduced.

**4** Gradually add the hot stock, a ladleful at a time. Stir constantly and add more liquid as the rice absorbs each addition. Increase the heat to medium so that the liquid bubbles. Cook for 20 minutes, or until all the liquid is absorbed and the rice is creamy.

**5** Add half the reserved mushroom soaking liquid and stir in the mushrooms. Season to taste and add more mushroom liquid, if necessary. Remove from the heat and stir in the remaining butter, the grated Parmesan, and chopped parsley. Serve at once.

# beet, dried cherry & red wine risotto

## ingredients

**SERVES 4–6**

6 oz/175 g/1$\frac{1}{2}$ cups dried
  sour cherries or dried
  cranberries
8 fl oz/225 ml/1 cup fruity red
  wine, such as Valpolicella
3 tbsp olive oil
1 large red onion,
  finely chopped
2 celery stalks, finely chopped
$\frac{1}{2}$ tsp dried thyme
1 garlic clove, finely chopped
12 oz/350 g/1$\frac{3}{4}$ cups
  Arborio rice
2 pints/1.2 liters/5 cups
  simmering chicken or
  vegetable stock
  (see page 18)
4 cooked fresh beet, diced
2 tbsp chopped fresh dill
2 tbsp snipped fresh chives
salt and pepper
2$\frac{1}{4}$ oz/60 g/generous $\frac{1}{2}$ cup
  freshly grated Parmesan
  cheese, to serve (optional)

## method

**1** Place the sour cherries in a pan with the wine and bring to a boil, then reduce the heat and let simmer for 2–3 minutes until slightly reduced. Remove from the heat and set aside.

**2** Heat the olive oil in a large, heavy-bottom pan over medium heat. Add the onion, celery, and thyme and cook, stirring occasionally, for 3 minutes, or until just starting to soften. Add the garlic and cook for 30 seconds. Reduce the heat, add the rice, and mix to coat in oil. Cook, stirring constantly, for 2–3 minutes, or until the grains are translucent.

**3** Gradually add the hot stock, a ladleful at a time. Stir constantly and add more liquid as the rice absorbs each addition. Increase the heat to medium so that the liquid bubbles. Cook for 20 minutes, or until the liquid is absorbed and the rice is creamy.

**4** Halfway through the risotto cooking time, remove the cherries from the wine with a slotted spoon and add to the risotto with the beet and half the wine. Continue adding the stock and the remaining wine.

**5** Stir in the dill and chives and season, if necessary. Serve with a sprinkling of grated Parmesan, if you like.

# side dishes

Rice makes a wonderful alternative to potatoes or bread as a filling accompaniment, and is so versatile that it can play a quiet supporting role to the main dish—or completely steal the show!

In China and Thailand, rice is eaten in vast quantities and cooked in endlessly inventive ways. A delicious and simple accompaniment to a Thai dish is Jasmine Rice with Lemon and Basil. Coconut milk is used in many dishes in this part of the world—Coconut Rice with Pineapple is rich and tasty, with a sprinkling of toasted coconut flakes to garnish.

Egg Fried Rice has become as popular in the Western world as it is in China, and cooked with vegetables and crispy onions is almost a meal in itself. Stir-fried rice and vegetable dishes are the labor-saving way to cook all your accompaniments in one pan, and retain all the nutrients, too.

Most nations have their version of a rice-based side dish. In Spain, rice is sometimes cooked with sherry, which gives it a rich flavor that goes well with roast veal, pork, or chicken. In the Caribbean, it is cooked with a cinnamon stick and a hot green chile, while Mexicans color their rice with plenty of fresh cilantro. In India, Rice with Warm Spices goes well with curries. It's time to experiment!

# fried rice with pork & shrimp

## ingredients

**SERVES 4**

3 tsp vegetable or peanut oil

1 egg, lightly beaten

$3^1/_2$ oz/100 g raw shrimp,
    shelled, deveined and cut
    into 2 pieces

$3^1/_2$ oz/100 g cha siu
    (barbecued pork),
    finely chopped

2 tbsp finely chopped scallion

7 oz/200 g/scant $1^1/_2$ cups
    cooked rice, chilled

1 tsp salt

## method

**1** In a preheated wok, heat 1 teaspoon of the oil and pour in the egg. Cook until scrambled. Remove and set aside.

**2** Add the remaining oil  to the wok and stir-fry the shrimp, cha siu, and scallion for about 2 minutes. Add the rice and salt, breaking up the rice into grains, and cook for an additional 2 minutes. Finally, stir in the cooked egg. Serve immediately.

# sushi rice

## ingredients

**SERVES 4**

9 oz/250 g/scant 1$^1$/$_4$ cups
   sushi rice
11$^1$/$_2$ fl oz/325 ml/generous
   1$^1$/$_4$ cups water
1 piece of dried kombu
   (edible kelp)
2 tbsp sushi rice seasoning

## method

**1** Wash the sushi rice under cold running water until the water running through it is clear, then drain the rice. Put the rice in a pan with the water and the kombu, then cover and bring to a boil as quickly as you can.

**2** Remove the kombu, then turn the heat down and let simmer for 10 minutes. Turn off the heat and let the rice stand for 15 minutes. Do not at any point take the lid off the pan once you have removed the kombu.

**3** Put the hot rice in a large, very shallow bowl and pour the sushi rice seasoning evenly over the surface of the rice. Use one hand to mix the seasoning carefully into the rice with quick cutting strokes using a spatula, and the other to fan the sushi rice in order to cool it quickly.

**4** The sushi rice should look shiny and be at room temperature when you are ready to use it.

# asian coconut rice

## ingredients

**SERVES 4**

2 tbsp vegetable oil

1 onion, chopped

14 oz/400 g/2 cups long grain
   rice, rinsed and drained

1 tbsp freshly chopped
   lemongrass

18 fl oz/500 ml/generous
   2$^1$/$_2$ cups coconut milk

14 fl oz/400 ml/1$^3$/$_4$ cups
   water

6 tbsp flaked coconut, toasted

## method

**1** Heat the oil in a large pan over low heat, add the onion, and cook, stirring frequently, for 3 minutes. Add the rice and lemongrass and cook, stirring, for an additional 2 minutes.

**2** Stir in the coconut milk and water and bring to a boil. Reduce the heat, cover, and let simmer for 20–25 minutes until all the liquid has been absorbed. If the rice grains have not cooked through, add a little more water and cook until tender and all the liquid has been absorbed.

**3** Remove from the heat and add half the flaked coconut. Stir gently. Sprinkle over the remaining coconut flakes and serve.

# golden rice

## ingredients

**SERVES 4**

1 tsp saffron threads

2 tbsp hot water

2 tbsp ghee or vegetable oil

3 onions, chopped

3 tbsp butter

1 tsp ground cumin

1 tsp ground cinnamon

1 tsp salt

$^1/_2$ tsp pepper

$^1/_2$ tsp paprika

3 bay leaves

14 oz/400 g/2 cups long-grain rice, rinsed and drained

about 1$^1/_2$ pints/850 ml/ 3$^1/_2$ cups vegetable stock or water

3$^1/_2$ oz/100 g/$^3/_4$ cup cashew halves, toasted

## method

**1** Put the saffron threads and hot water into a small bowl and set aside to soak.

**2** Meanwhile, heat the ghee in a large pan over low heat, add the onions, and cook, stirring frequently, for 5 minutes. Add the butter, cumin, cinnamon, salt, pepper, paprika, and bay leaves and cook, stirring, for 2 minutes,then add the rice and cook, stirring, for 3 minutes. Add the saffron and its soaking liquid and pour in the stock.

**3** Bring to a boil, then reduce the heat, cover, and let simmer for 20–25 minutes until all the liquid has been absorbed. If the rice grains have not cooked through, add a little more stock and cook until tender and all the liquid has been absorbed.

**4** Remove from the heat and remove and discard the bay leaves. Taste and adjust the seasoning, if necessary. Add the cashews and stir well. Serve hot.

# sherry rice

## ingredients

**SERVES 4–6**

2 tbsp olive oil

1 large red onion, chopped finely

1 large garlic clove, crushed

14 oz/400 g/2 cups Spanish short-grain rice

8 fl oz/225 ml/1 cup amontillado sherry

1³/₄ pints/1 liter/4 cups fresh chicken stock, hot

pinch of cayenne pepper

salt and pepper

## method

**1** Heat the oil in a shallow, heavy-bottom flameproof casserole. Add the onions and cook for 3 minutes, then add the garlic and cook for an additional 2 minutes, or until the onions are soft, but not brown.

**2** Rinse the rice until the water runs clear. Drain, then add to the casserole and stir until it is coated in the oil. Add all but 2 tablespoons of the sherry and let it bubble. Pour in the stock with the cayenne and salt and pepper to taste and bring to a boil. Reduce the heat and let simmer for 20 minutes, uncovered and without stirring, until most of the stock is absorbed and small holes appear on the surface.

**3** Turn off the heat under the rice, sprinkle with the remaining sherry, cover, and let stand for 10 minutes until all the liquid is absorbed.

# jasmine rice with lemon & basil

## ingredients

**SERVES 4**

14 oz/400 g/2 cups jasmine rice

1 1/4 pints/725 ml/ 3 1/4 cups water

finely grated rind of 1/2 lemon

2 tbsp shredded fresh basil, to serve

## method

**1** Wash the rice in several changes of cold water until the water runs clear. Bring 1 1/4 pints/725 ml/3 1/4 cups of water to a boil in a large pan, then add the rice.

**2** Return to a rolling boil. Turn the heat to a low simmer, then cover the pan and simmer for an additional 12 minutes. Remove the pan from the heat and let stand, covered, for 10 minutes.

**3** Fluff up the rice with a fork, then stir in the lemon rind. Serve sprinkled with shredded basil.

# coconut rice with pineapple

## ingredients

**SERVES 4**

7 oz/200 g/1 cup
   long-grain rice
16 fl oz/450 ml/generous
   2 cups coconut milk
2 lemongrass stems
6 fl oz/175 ml/generous
   3/4 cup water
2 slices fresh pineapple,
   peeled and diced
2 tbsp toasted coconut
chili sauce, to serve

## method

**1** Wash the rice in several changes of cold water until the water runs clear. Place in a large pan with the coconut milk.

**2** Place the lemongrass on a counter and bruise it by hitting firmly with a rolling pin or mallet. Add to the pan with the rice and coconut milk.

**3** Add the water and bring to a boil. Reduce the heat, then cover the pan tightly and simmer gently for 15 minutes. Remove the pan from the heat and fluff up the rice with a fork.

**4** Remove the lemongrass and stir in the pineapple. Sprinkle with toasted coconut and serve immediately with chili sauce.

# caribbean cook-up rice

## ingredients

**SERVES 4**

2 tbsp butter

1 onion, chopped

1 garlic clove, finely chopped

1 carrot, chopped

14 oz/400 g canned gunga
    peas, drained and rinsed

1 cinnamon stick

1 fresh thyme sprig

1 pint/600 ml/2$^1$/$_2$ cups
    vegetable stock

2 oz/55 g block creamed
    coconut

1 fresh green chile, seeded
    and chopped

salt and pepper

14 oz/400 g/2 cups
    long-grain rice

## method

**1** Melt the butter in a large, heavy-bottom skillet or flameproof casserole. Add the onion and garlic and cook over low heat, stirring occasionally, for 5 minutes, or until softened.

**2** Add the carrot, gunga peas, cinnamon stick, thyme, vegetable stock, coconut, and chile, stir well, and season to taste with salt and pepper. Bring to a boil, stirring frequently.

**3** Add the rice and return to a boil, then reduce the heat, cover, and let simmer for 15 minutes, or until the rice is tender and all the liquid has been absorbed. Remove and discard the thyme sprig and cinnamon stick, then fluff up the rice with a fork. Transfer to individual serving dishes and serve at once.

# saffron rice with green vegetables

## ingredients

**SERVES 4–6**

large pinch saffron threads
2 pints/1.2 liters/5 cups
    vegetable stock, hot
2 tbsp extra-virgin olive oil
1 large onion, chopped finely
1 large garlic clove, crushed
14 oz/400 g/2 cups short-grain
    Spanish rice
$3^1/_2$ oz/100 g thin green
    beans, chopped
salt and pepper
$3^1/_2$ oz/100 g/scant 1 cup
    frozen peas
flat-leaf parsley, to garnish

## method

**1** Put the saffron threads in a small heatproof bowl and add the hot vegetable stock, then set aside to infuse.

**2** Meanwhile, heat the oil in a shallow, heavy-bottom flameproof casserole over medium–high heat. Add the onions and cook for about 3 minutes, then add the garlic and cook for an additional 2 minutes, or until the onions are soft, but not brown.

**3** Rinse the rice until the water runs clear. Drain, then add with the beans and stir until they are coated with oil. Pour in the stock with salt and pepper to taste and bring to a boil. Reduce the heat and let simmer for 12 minutes, uncovered, and without stirring.

**4** Gently stir in the peas and continue simmering for 8 minutes until the liquid has been absorbed and the beans and peas are tender. Taste and adjust the seasoning. Garnish with the parsley and serve.

# stir-fried rice with green vegetables

## ingredients

SERVES 4

8 oz/225 g/generous 1 cup
   jasmine rice
2 tbsp vegetable or peanut oil
1 tbsp Thai green curry paste
6 scallions, sliced
2 garlic cloves, crushed
1 zucchini, cut into thin sticks
4 oz/115 g yard-long beans
6 oz/175 g asparagus,
   trimmed
1 tbsp fish sauce
3–4 fresh Thai basil leaves

## method

1 Cook the rice in lightly salted boiling water for 12–15 minutes, drain well, then cool thoroughly and chill overnight.

2 Heat the oil in a wok and stir-fry the curry paste for 1 minute. Add the scallions and garlic and stir-fry for 1 minute.

3 Add the zucchini, beans, and asparagus, and stir-fry for 3–4 minutes, until just tender. Break up the rice and add it to the wok. Cook, stirring constantly for 2–3 minutes, until the rice is hot. Stir in the fish sauce and basil leaves. Serve hot.

# egg fu yung

## ingredients

**SERVES 4–6**

2 eggs

$1/2$ tsp salt

pinch of white pepper

1 tsp melted butter

2 tbsp vegetable or peanut oil

1 tsp finely chopped garlic

1 small onion, finely sliced

1 green bell pepper, finely
   sliced

1 lb/450 g/4 cups cooked
   rice, chilled

1 tbsp light soy sauce

1 tbsp finely chopped scallion

5 oz/140 g/1 cup bean
   sprouts, trimmed

2 drops of sesame oil

## method

**1** Beat the eggs with the salt and pepper. Heat the butter in a pan and pour in the eggs. Cook as an omelet, until set, then remove from the pan and cut into slivers.

**2** In a preheated wok or deep pan, heat the oil and stir-fry the garlic until fragrant. Add the onion and stir-fry for 1 minute, then add the green bell pepper and stir for 1 more minute. Stir in the rice and when the grains are separated, stir in the light soy sauce and cook for 1 minute.

**3** Add the scallion and egg strips and stir well, then finally add the bean sprouts and sesame oil. Stir-fry for 1 minute and serve.

# egg fried rice

## ingredients

SERVES 4

5$^1$/$_2$ oz/150 g/generous
$^1$/$_2$ cup long-grain rice

3 eggs, beaten

2 tbsp vegetable oil

2 garlic cloves, crushed

4 scallions, chopped

125 g/4$^1$/$_2$ oz/generous
1 cup cooked peas

1 tbsp light soy sauce

pinch of salt

shredded scallion, to garnish

## method

**1** Cook the rice in a pan of boiling water for 10–12 minutes until almost cooked, but not soft. Drain well, rinse under cold running water and drain thoroughly.

**2** Place the beaten eggs in a pan and cook over a low heat, stirring constantly until softly scrambled. Remove the pan from the heat and reserve.

**3** Preheat a wok over a medium heat. Add the oil and swirl it around to coat the sides of the wok. When the oil is hot, add the garlic, scallions, and peas and sauté, stirring occasionally, for 1–2 minutes.

**4** Stir the rice into the mixture in the wok, mixing to combine. Add the eggs, soy sauce and salt to the wok and stir to mix the egg in thoroughly.

**5** Transfer to serving dishes and serve garnished with the shredded scallion.

# egg-fried rice with vegetables & crispy onions

## ingredients

**SERVES 4**

4 tbsp vegetable or peanut oil

2 garlic cloves, chopped finely

2 fresh red chiles, seeded and chopped

4 oz/115 g mushrooms, sliced

2 oz/50 g snow peas, halved

2 oz/50 g baby corn, halved

3 tbsp Thai soy sauce

1 tbsp jaggery or soft light brown sugar

few Thai basil leaves

12 oz/350 g/3 cups long-grain rice, cooked and cooled

2 eggs, beaten

2 onions, sliced

## method

**1** Heat half the oil in a wok or large skillet and sauté the garlic and chiles for 2–3 minutes. Add the mushrooms, snow peas, and corn, and stir-fry for 2–3 minutes before adding the soy sauce, sugar, and basil. Stir in the rice.

**2** Push the mixture to one side of the wok and add the eggs to the bottom. Stir until lightly set before combining into the rice mixture.

**3** Heat the remaining oil in another skillet and sauté the onions until crispy and brown. Serve the rice topped with the onions.

# stir-fried rice with egg strips

## ingredients

**SERVES 4**

2 tbsp peanut oil

1 egg, beaten with 1 tsp water

1 garlic clove, finely chopped

1 small onion, finely chopped

1 tbsp Thai red curry paste

10 oz/300 g/1¼ cups
  long-grain rice, cooked
  and cooled

2 oz/55 g/½ cup
  cooked peas

1 tbsp Thai fish sauce

2 tbsp tomato ketchup

2 tbsp chopped cilantro

## to garnish

fresh red chile flowers
cucumber slices

## method

**1** To make chile flowers for the garnish, hold the stem of a fresh red chile with your fingertips and use a small, sharp, pointed knife to cut a slit down the length from near the stem end to the tip. Turn the chile about a quarter turn and make another cut. Repeat to make a total of 4 cuts, then scrape out the seeds. Cut each "petal" again in half, or into fourths, to make 8–16 petals. Place the chile flower in ice water.

**2** Heat 1 teaspoon of the oil in a preheated wok or large skillet. Pour in the egg mixture, swirling it to coat the wok evenly and make a thin layer. When set and golden, remove the egg from the wok and roll up. Set aside.

**3** Add the remaining oil to the wok. Add the garlic and onion and stir-fry for 1 minute. Add the curry paste, then stir in the rice and peas.

**4** Stir in the fish sauce, ketchup, and cilantro. Remove the wok from the heat and pile the rice on to a serving dish. Slice the egg roll into spiral strips, without unrolling, and use to garnish the rice. Add the cucumber slices and chile flowers. Serve hot.

# rice with lime

## ingredients

**SERVES 4**

2 tbsp vegetable oil

1 small onion, finely chopped

3 garlic cloves, finely chopped

6 oz/175 g mixed long-grain
and wild rice

16 fl oz/450 ml/2 cups
chicken or vegetable stock

juice of 1 lime

1 tbsp chopped fresh cilantro

## method

**1** Heat the oil in a heavy-based pan or flameproof casserole. Add the onion and garlic and cook gently, stirring occasionally, for 2 minutes. Add the rice and cook for an additional minute, stirring. Pour in the stock, increase the heat and bring the rice to a boil. Reduce the heat to a very low simmer.

**2** Cover the pan and cook the rice for about 10 minutes or until the rice is just tender and all the liquid has been absorbed. Sprinkle in the lime juice and fork the rice to fluff up and to mix the juice in. Sprinkle with the cilantro and serve.

# green rice

## ingredients

**SERVES 4**

1 onion, halved and unpeeled

6–8 large garlic cloves,
   unpeeled

1 large mild chile, or 1 green
   bell pepper and 1 small
   green chile

1 bunch fresh cilantro leaves,
   chopped

8 fl oz/125 ml/1 cup chicken
   or vegetable stock

3 fl oz/80 ml/$^1/_3$ cup
   vegetable or olive oil

6 oz/175 g/1 cup
   long-grain rice

salt and pepper

fresh cilantro sprig, to garnish

## method

**1** Heat a heavy-based ungreased skillet and cook the onion, garlic, chile, and bell pepper, if using, until lightly charred on all sides, including the cut sides of the onions. Cover and let cool.

**2** When cool enough to handle, remove the seeds and skin from the chile and bell pepper, if using. Chop the flesh. Remove the skins from the onion and garlic and chop finely. Place the vegetables in a food processor with the cilantro leaves and stock, then process until a smooth thin purée forms.

**3** Heat the oil in a heavy-bottom pan and fry the rice until it is glistening and lightly browned in places, stirring to prevent it from burning. Add the purée, cover and cook over a medium–low heat for 10–15 minutes until the rice is just tender.

**4** Fluff up the rice with a fork, then cover and stand for about 5 minutes. Adjust the seasoning, garnish with a sprig of cilantro and serve.

# rice with black beans

## ingredients

**SERVES 4**

1 onion, chopped

5 garlic cloves, chopped

8 fl oz/225 ml/1 cup chicken
   or vegetable stock

2 tbsp vegetable oil

6oz/175 g/1 cup
   long-grain rice

1 cup liquid from cooking
   black beans (including
   some black beans, too)

$1/2$ tsp ground cumin

salt and pepper

## to garnish

3–5 scallions, thinly sliced

2 tbsp chopped fresh cilantro
   leaves

## method

**1** Put the onion in a blender with the garlic and stock and blend until the consistency of a chunky sauce.

**2** Heat the oil in a heavy-based pan and cook the rice until it is golden. Add the onion mixture, with the cooking liquid from the black beans (and any beans, too). Add the cumin, with salt and pepper to taste.

**3** Cover and cook over a medium-low heat for about 10 minutes until the rice is just tender. It should be a grayish color and taste delicious.

**4** Fluff up the rice with a fork, and leave to rest about 5 minutes, covered. Serve sprinkled with scallions and cilantro.

# rice with warm spices

## ingredients

**SERVES 4**

6 oz/175 g/generous 1 cup
   basmati rice

1 pint/600 ml/2$^1$/$_2$ cups water

2 whole cloves

4 cardamom pods, lightly
   crushed

1 cinnamon stick

pinch of saffron threads,
   lightly crushed

salt

2 tbsp lime juice

1 tbsp finely grated lime rind

2oz/55 g/$^1$/$_3$ cup golden
   raisins

1 oz/25 g/scant $^1$/$_2$ cup
   pistachios, coarsely
   chopped

## method

**1** Rinse the rice in several changes of water and let soak for 10 minutes. Drain well.

**2** Pour the water into a large, heavy-bottom pan, add the cloves, cardamoms, cinnamon stick, saffron threads, and a pinch of salt and bring to a boil over medium heat. Add the rice and return to a boil. Reduce the heat, cover tightly, and let simmer for 10–15 minutes. Remove the pan from the heat and let stand, still covered, for 5 minutes.

**3** Uncover the rice and fluff up the grains with a fork, then gently stir in the lime juice, lime rind, golden raisins, and pistachios. Taste and adjust the seasoning, if necessary, and serve.

# desserts

We tend to associate rice with savory dishes, but it also lends itself beautifully to desserts. They can be cooked on the hob, baked in the oven, or even steamed, and are served hot or chilled.

Different nations each have their own way of flavoring their rice puddings, turning what is essentially the same dish into something unique. The Spanish, for example, add orange and lemon rinds and a vanilla bean, as well as milk and heavy cream, making a creamy dessert with a tempting aroma, which is eaten as soon as it's cooked or chilled. The Greek version is similar, but eaten cold with a generous sprinkling of cinnamon. In Thailand, the rice is cooked in coconut milk, flavored with spices, and eaten hot. Indian rice pudding is made with basmati rice, which has its own distinctive flavor. The Chinese make a wonderful steamed rice pudding with the intriguing name of Eight-Treasures Sweet Rice Cake. It's made with glutinous rice and dried fruit and flavored with lotus seeds, and is eaten in slices, unlike the winter rice pudding which again is made with dried fruits, but is cooked in a pan.

And for those of you who like a little chocolate with their dessert, there's a treat for you—a truly sumptuous chilled chocolate rice dessert, with just a touch of brandy!

# spanish rice pudding

## ingredients

**SERVES 4–6**

1 large orange

1 lemon

1³/₄ pints/1 liter/4 cups milk

9 oz/250 g/scant 1¹/₄ cups
Spanish short-grain rice

3³/₄ oz/100 g/generous
¹/₂ cup superfine sugar

1 vanilla bean, split

pinch of salt

4 fl oz/125 ml/¹/₂ cup
heavy cream

brown sugar, to serve
(optional)

## method

**1** Finely grate the rinds from the orange and lemon and set aside. Rinse a heavy-bottom pan with cold water, but do not dry it.

**2** Put the milk and rice in the pan over medium–high heat and bring to a boil. Reduce the heat, stir in the superfine sugar, vanilla bean, orange and lemon rinds, and salt and let simmer, stirring frequently, until the pudding is thick and creamy and the rice grains are tender. This can take up to 30 minutes, depending on how wide the pan is.

**3** Remove the vanilla bean and stir in the cream. Serve immediately, sprinkled with brown sugar, if desired, or let cool completely, cover, and let chill until required. (The pudding will thicken as it cools, so stir in extra milk, if necessary.)

# creamy rice pudding

## ingredients

**SERVES 4**

1 tbsp butter, for greasing

3 oz/85 g/$^1$/$_2$ cup
    golden raisins

5 tbsp superfine sugar

3$^1$/$_4$ oz/90 g/$^2$/$_3$ cup sweet rice

2 pints/1.2 liters/5 cups milk

1 tsp vanilla extract

finely grated zest of 1 large
    lemon

pinch of nutmeg

chopped pistachios,
    to decorate

## method

**1** Grease a 1$^1$/$_2$-pint/850-ml/3$^1$/$_2$-cup ovenproof dish with the butter.

**2** Put the golden raisins, sugar, and rice into a mixing bowl, then stir in the milk and vanilla extract. Transfer to the greased ovenproof dish, sprinkle over the grated lemon zest and the nutmeg, then bake in a preheated oven, 325°F/160°C, for 2$^1$/$_2$ hours.

**3** Remove from the oven and transfer to individual serving bowls. Decorate with chopped pistachios and serve.

# spicy rice pudding

## ingredients

**SERVES 4**

14 fl oz/400 ml/1³/₄ cups
    canned coconut milk

5 fl oz/150 ml/²/₃ cup milk

2 oz/55 g/generous ¹/₄ cup
    light soft brown sugar

2 oz/55 g/generous ¹/₄ cup
    short-grain rice

2 tsp allspice

1 oz butter

1 tsp ground cinnamon

## method

**1** Pour the coconut milk and milk in a pan and heat gently. Add the sugar and stir until it has dissolved.

**2** Add the rice and allspice and gradually bring to a boil. Let simmer gently, stirring frequently, for 45–60 minutes, until thickened.

**3** Stir in the butter, and once it has melted, serve immediately, sprinkled with cinnamon.

# greek rice pudding

## ingredients

**SERVES 4**

4¹/₂ oz/125 g/²/₃ cup
    short-grain rice
¹/₂ pint/300 ml/1¹/₄ cups
    water
1 tbsp cornstarch
1 pint/600 ml/2¹/₂ cups
    whole milk
3 oz/85 g/¹/₃ cup superfine
    sugar
1 tsp vanilla extract or finely
    grated rind of 1 large lemon
ground cinnamon, to serve

## method

**1** Put the rice in a pan and add the water. Bring to the boil then simmer for 12–15 minutes, stirring occasionally, until the water has been absorbed. Meanwhile, in a small bowl, blend the cornstarch with 2 tablespoons of the milk.

**2** Add the remaining milk to the rice, return to the boil then simmer for 20–25 minutes, stirring frequently, until the rice is very soft and most of the liquid has been absorbed. Stir in the sugar, vanilla or lemon rind, and the cornstarch mixture, return to the boil then simmer for a further 5 minutes, stirring.

**3** Spoon the rice mixture into individual serving dishes and let cool. Serve cold, sprinkled generously with cinnamon.

# indian rice pudding

## ingredients

**SERVES 8–10**

2³/3 oz/75 g/scant ¹/2 cup
    basmati rice

2 pints/1.2 liters/5 cups milk

8 tbsp sugar

varq (silver leaf) or chopped
    pistachios, to decorate

## method

**1** Rinse the rice under cold running water and place in a large, heavy-bottom pan. Add 1 pint/600 ml/2¹/2 cups of the milk and bring to a boil over very low heat. Cook until the milk has been completely absorbed by the rice, stirring occasionally.

**2** Remove the pan from the heat. Mash the rice, making swift, round movements in the pan, for at least 5 minutes.

**3** Gradually add the remaining milk. Return the pan to the heat and bring to a boil over low heat, stirring occasionally.

**4** Add the sugar and cook, stirring constantly, for 7–10 minutes, or until the mixture is quite thick in consistency.

**5** Transfer the rice pudding to a heatproof serving bowl. Decorate with varq (silver leaf) or chopped pistachios and serve.

# thai rice pudding

## ingredients

**SERVES 4**

2²/₃ oz/75 g/scant ¹/₂ cup
   short-grain rice

2 tbsp palm sugar

1 cardamom pod, split

10 fl oz/300 ml/1¹/₄ cups
   coconut milk

5 fl oz/150 ml/²/₃ cup water

3 eggs

4 oz/115 g/generous ³/₄ cup
   coconut cream

1¹/₂ tbsp superfine sugar

sweetened coconut flakes, to
   decorate

fresh fruits, to serve

## method

**1** Place the rice and palm sugar in a pan. Remove the seeds from the cardamom pod and place in a mortar. Crush the seeds using a pestle, then add to the pan. Stir in the coconut milk and water.

**2** Bring to a boil, stirring to dissolve the sugar. Reduce the heat and let simmer, uncovered, stirring occasionally, for 20 minutes, or until the rice is tender and most of the liquid is absorbed.

**3** Spoon the rice into 4 individual ovenproof dishes and spread evenly. Place the dishes in a wide roasting pan and pour in enough water to come halfway up the sides.

**4** Beat the eggs, coconut cream, and superfine sugar together in a bowl. Spoon over the rice. Cover with foil and bake in a preheated oven, 350°F/180°C, for 45–50 minutes, or until set.

**5** Turn out the puddings onto individual serving dishes and decorate with coconut flakes. Serve warm or cold with fresh fruit.

# winter rice pudding with dried fruits

## ingredients

**SERVES 6–8**

1 tbsp peanuts

1 tbsp pine nuts

1 tbsp lotus seeds

8 oz/225 g mixed dried fruits
(raisins, kumquats,
prunes, dates, etc.)

3$^1$/$_2$ pints/2 liters/8$^3$/$_4$ cups
water

4 oz/115g/generous
$^1$/$_2$ cup sugar

8 oz/225 ml/generous 1 cup
glutinous rice, soaked in
cold water for at least
2 hours

## method

**1** Soak the peanuts, pine nuts, and lotus seeds in a bowl of cold water for at least 1 hour. Soak the dried fruits as necessary. Chop all larger fruits into small pieces.

**2** Bring the water to a boil in a pan, then add the sugar and stir until dissolved. Add the drained rice, nuts, and lotus seeds and mixed dried fruits. Bring back to a boil. Cover and simmer over very low heat for 1 hour, stirring frequently.

# eight-treasures sweet rice cake

## ingredients

**SERVES 6–8**

8 oz/225g/generous 1 cup
glutinous rice, soaked in
cold water for at least
2 hours

3¹/₂ oz/100 g/¹/₂ cup sugar

2 tablespoons shortening

2 dried kumquats, finely
chopped

3 prunes, finely chopped

5 dried red dates, soaked for
20 minutes in warm water,
then finely chopped

1 tsp raisins

12 lotus seeds (if using dried
seeds, soak in warm
water for at least 1 hour)

3¹/₂ oz/100 g sweet red
bean paste

## method

**1** Steam the glutinous rice for 20 minutes, or
until soft. Set aside. When the rice is cool, mix
in the sugar and shortening by hand to form a
sticky mass.

**2** Arrange the dried fruits and seeds in the
base of a clear pudding basin. Top with half
the rice, then press down tightly and smooth
the top.

**3** Spread the bean paste on top of the rice,
and top with the remaining rice. Press down
and smooth the top.

**4** Steam for 20 minutes and let cool slightly,
then turn out onto a plate. Cut into small slices
at the table.

# chocolate rice pudding

## ingredients

**SERVES 8**

3¹/₂ oz/100 g/¹/₂ cup long-
grain white rice

pinch of salt

1 pint/300 ml/2 ¹/₂ cups milk

3¹/₂ oz/100 g/¹/₂ cup
granulated sugar

7 oz/200 g semisweet or
bittersweet chocolate,
chopped

4 tbsp butter, diced

1 tsp vanilla extract

2 tbsp brandy

6 fl oz/175 ml/³/₄ cup
heavy cream

whipped cream, for piping
(optional)

chocolate curls, to decorate
(optional)

## method

**1** Bring a pan of water to the boil. Sprinkle in the rice and add the salt. Reduce the heat and simmer gently for 15–20 minutes, or until the rice is just tender. Drain the rice, rinse, and drain again.

**2** Heat the milk and sugar in a large heavy-bottom pan over medium heat until the sugar dissolves, stirring frequently. Add the chocolate and butter to the pan and stir until melted and smooth.

**3** Stir in the cooked rice and reduce the heat to low. Cover and let simmer, stirring occasionally, for 30 minutes, until the milk is absorbed and the mixture thickened. Stir in the vanilla extract and brandy. Remove from the heat and let cool to room temperature.

**4** Using an electric mixer, beat the cream until soft peaks form. Stir one heaped spoonful of the cream into the chocolate rice mixture to lighten it then fold in the remaining cream.

**5** Spoon into glass serving dishes, cover, and let chill for about 2 hours. If wished, decorate with piped whipped cream and top with chocolate curls. Serve cold.

# chilled rice pudding

## ingredients

**SERVES 4**

4 oz/115 g/$^1/_2$ cup
    short-grain rice
10 fl oz/300 ml/1$^1/_4$ cups milk
10 fl oz/300 ml/1$^1/_4$ cups
    heavy cream, plus extra
    for decoration
2 oz/55 g/$^1/_4$ cup superfine
    sugar
1 tbsp grated lemon rind
1 tsp ground cinnamon, plus
    extra for dusting

## method

**1** Rinse the rice well and place in the top of a double boiler with the milk, cream, sugar, lemon rind, and ground cinnamon. Set over a pan of gently simmering water, cover, and cook, stirring occasionally, for 55 minutes, or until most of the liquid has been absorbed and the rice is tender.

**2** Remove the pan from the heat and transfer the rice mixture into individual dishes or cups. Let cool, then cover and chill in the refrigerator for 2–3 hours, or until set.

**3** To serve, whip the extra heavy cream, decorate each dish with a swirl, and lightly dust with cinnamon.